—— THE ——

LOST EMPIRES

AND **VANISHED**

RACES

OF
THE **BOOK** OF

MORMON

THE

LOST EMPIRES

AND **VANISHED**

RACES

OF THE **BOOK** OF

MORMON

PHYLLIS CAROL OLIVE

CFI

AN IMPRINT OF CEDAR FORT, INC.
SPRINGVILLE, UTAH

The views expressed within this work are the sole responsibility of the author and do not necessarily reflect the position of Cedar Fort, Inc., or any other entity.

ISBN 13: 978-1-4621-1135-0

Published by CFI, an imprint of Cedar Fort, Inc., 2373 W. 700 S., Springville, UT 84663
Distributed by Cedar Fort, Inc., www.cedarfort.com

LIBRARY OF CONGRESS CATALOGING-IN-PUBLICATION DATA

Olive, Phyllis Carol, author.
The lost empires and vanished races of the Book of Mormon / Phyllis Carol Olive.
    pages cm
Includes bibliographical references and index.
ISBN 978-1-4621-1135-0 (alk. paper)
1. Book of Mormon--Antiquities. 2. Book of Mormon--Geography. 3. America--Antiquities.
I. Title.

BX8627.O45 2013
289.3'22--dc23

                            2012044963

Cover design by Erica Dixon
Cover design © 2013 by Lyle Mortimer
Edited and typeset by Melissa J. Caldwell

Printed in the United States of America

10 9 8 7 6 5 4 3 2 1

Printed on acid-free paper

Also by Phyllis Carol Olive

The Lost Lands of the Book of Mormon
The Lost Tribe of the Book of Mormon
The Millennium

Contents

—⟨ Preface ⟩—

In the Doctrine and Covenants, we are counseled to gain knowledge and to learn out of the best books such things as history and a knowledge of all the perplexing things that transpired among the nations over the course of the world's long history. We read:

> Teach ye diligently and my grace shall attend you, that you may be instructed more perfectly in theory, in principle, in doctrine, in the law of the gospel, in all things that pertain unto the kingdom of God, that are expedient for you to understand; of things both in heaven and in the earth, and under the earth; things which have been, things which are, things which must shortly come to pass; things which are at home, things which are abroad; the wars and the perplexities of the nations, and the judgments which are on the land; and a knowledge also of countries and of kingdoms. (Doctrine and Covenants 88:78–79)

> And, verily I say unto you, that it is my will that you should hasten to translate my scriptures, and to obtain a knowledge

of history, and of countries, and of kingdoms, of laws of God and man, and all this for the salvation of Zion. Amen. (Doctrine and Covenants 93:53)

What better things can those in America learn than the history of nations that have lived on the American continent throughout the centuries—what brought them to greatness, what caused their downfall, and what can be learned from the past.

⁓ Introduction ⁓

The Book of Mormon is more than a history book of two ancient civilizations; it testifies of the visit of Jesus Christ to the promised land after his death and resurrection. Moreover, it identifies through clues and keys the covenant land of Joseph, the favorite son of Jacob, who was sold into Egypt by his brothers.

The following work is provided to help identify Joseph's covenant land—America. This work will also identify a territory in western New York that fits the geographical description provided in the Book of Mormon remarkably well as well as identify the Lamanites—Lehi's lost and forgotten children who have continued to flourish in land long after the destruction of their Nephite brothers. President Ezra Taft Benson spoke of the many events that have transpired in this favored land. He said:

> Many great events have transpired in this land of destiny. This was the place where Adam dwelt; this was the place where the Garden of Eden was; it was here that Adam met with a body of high priests at Adam-ondi-Ahman shortly before his death and gave them his final blessings, and the

place to which he will go to meet the leaders of his people (D&C 107:53–57). This was the place of three former civilizations: that of Adam, that of the Jaredites, and that of the Nephites. This was also the place where our Heavenly Father and his Son, Jesus Christ, appeared to Joseph Smith, inaugurating the last dispensation.

The Lord has also decreed that this land should be "the place of the New Jerusalem, which should come down out of heaven, and the holy sanctuary of the Lord" (Ether 13:3). Here is our nation's destiny! To serve God's eternal purposes and to prepare this land and people for America's eventual destiny, He "established the constitution of this land, by the hands of wise men whom [He] raised up unto this very purpose, and redeemed the land by the shedding of blood" (D&C 101:80).[1]

The lands the Savior walked during his visit to the Nephites in this promised land of America are just as sacred as those he walked in the Old World and are worth searching for, for once they are discovered not only will the saga played out in the Book of Mormon come to life, but we will finally learn what happened to Lehi's descendants, the Lamanites, and how they fared through the centuries. Much of their history, which until now has only been hinted at to us, can now be pieced together, with each of the chapters that follow, fitting together new pieces of the puzzle.

Hebrew scholar Vincent Coon said:

> Some wish to avoid the so called "Book of Mormon geography controversy" unique to the Mormon community. Statements are parroted to the effect that, "it hasn't been revealed" or "it's not pertinent to my personal salvation." The truth is, the subject is about much more than geography. It is about covenant lands which matter to God and to the Israelites, and which should also matter to the Gentiles. Those who turn to the scriptures may come to see that the Lord has already placed in them keys for identifying the genuine lands

of Israel's inheritance. Like the prayerful Enos, some may find their hearts and understanding growing beyond concern for personal salvation. They may begin to take an interest in things relevant to the ancient and long dispersed covenant people of the Lord.

Phyllis Olive's setting for the covenant lands of the Book of Mormon is the most scripturally compatible of any proposed since the earliest days of the Restoration. Olive has avoided the temptation to exaggerate the scale of Book of Mormon lands or to locate them in places featured in popular travel logs. According to Olive, ancient America was ethnically diverse, even cosmopolitan. This position is in line with views set forth in nineteenth-century works on the "Mound Builders." Joseph Smith himself cited the best of these sources in his defense of the Book of Mormon.[2]

Part One

The Ancient Setting

1

Ancient Mariners

As the newly formed nations of the post-Flood world began to rebuild and various cultures emerged in different parts of the world, people became fascinated by tales of diverse cultures and the riches they produced. Thus, they constructed roads to facilitate trade. Water transport, however, proved the best mode of travel, for distances were greatly reduced, and ships could carry much more cargo than even the heaviest laden caravan. In this way, China gathered the wealth from the trade of their spices and stones and precious silk fabrics, which they sold for gold in the west. India gathered pearls and other precious stones and sold them to merchants from the east. Rome gathered goods from the East and sold it for wheat to feed its masses. And so it went from generation to generation as people and nations became better acquainted with one another and what each had to offer. And then stories began to filter in that the Inca in faraway Peru had gold and plants that grew in their jungles that could be made into various drugs. Thus, even longer voyages were made and kept secret so the precious trade routes to these ports would not be discovered, thereby diminishing any competition for precious cargos.

The Minoans initially ruled the seas. After came the Phoenicians, a mix of a number of races, including Canaanites. In fact, modern historians still often refer to the Phoenicians as Canaanites. Yet many now claim the original Phoenician seamen were red-headed Scythians, who eventually included the Danites of Israelite fame. E. Raymond Capt maintains that Danite Israelites went to sea with the Phoenicians as early as 1296 BC. Phoenician Tyre, along the east coast of the Mediterranean, was almost exclusively in Israelite power during the days of Solomon, and was under the control of the northern Tribes of Dan, Naphtali, Zebulon, Issachar, and Asher.

The Phoenicians were a technologically advanced people. In fact, they are known as the greatest seafaring merchants of the ancient world. Solomon employed their ships to form his navy and procure the precious resources he needed to build his temple. The ships of the Danites/Phoenicians were huge and had two to five rows of oars on each side. According to Julius Caesar, they were bigger, faster, and more maneuverable than even Roman ships. They are described in 1 Kings 22:48, as the largest seagoing vessels known to the Semitic world. Not only did they sail the Mediterranean, but they also circumnavigated Africa and sailed the open seas to Britain and Scandinavia, with enough evidence to suggest they also made it to America.

Walter Baucum referred to an account that had Phoenicians from Carthage transporting "30,000 men and women in 60 ships on a colonizing venture beyond the Pillars of Hercules," which some speculate took them to west Africa. However, he argues that it might well have been across the Atlantic to America in 500–480 BC, when large-scale migration and colonization by sea was taking place.[1]

Evidence of long-distance trade by ancient Israelites appears at Los Lunas, near Albuquerque, New Mexico, where a version of the Ten Commandments was found engraved on a rock. A similar inscription was found on a stone tablet in a burial mound at Newark, Ohio. Controversy still surrounds their early dates and style writing, but the fact that they contained the Ten Commandments shows possible ties to the Hebrews.[2]

One legend has it that a seafaring branch of Hebrews helped their inland Hebrew brothers escape from Egypt during the Exodus, and when Pharaoh sent troops to destroy them, God sent a rare east wind that carried them to the Iberian Peninsula, or Spain, where they became some of the greatest seafaring men of their day. As a reward, God promised to bless their ships and those of their children and their children's children. Such a direct blessing allowed them to sail the seven seas and prosper. Those who merged with the Danites in Denmark becoming the greatest sea power of their time. Thus, we can suppose they were perfectly capable of braving the Atlantic and making their way to America. The Danites are said to have been experts in the production of bronze and thus would have been much aware of the lucrative copper mines around Lake Superior. They likely set up permanent settlement sites in various regions around the Great Lakes and along the

Atlantic coast, where their ships were waiting to transport the copper home, with King Solomon likely their biggest customer.

The script found an ancient site in New Hampshire,

Phoenician ship

referred to as "Mystery Hill," was dedicated to the Phoenician god Baal. Other inscriptions at the site indicate that it was inhabited or frequented by ancient Celts, Iberians, and Phoenicians over many centuries. Barry Fell, who deciphered many of the inscriptions in New England, believed the European Celts built the megalithic chamber found in the area but welcomed Phoenician mariners and "permitted [them] to worship at the Celtic sanctuaries and to make dedications to their own gods in their own language."[3]

The Danites/Phoenicians carried the seed of Israel far and wide, and not surprisingly, for they were destined to do so. When Moses gave his final blessing to the children of Israel, he prophesied that Dan would be as a lion's whelp: who should "leap from Bashan" (Deuteronomy 33:22), suggesting his tribe would be a warlike people who would journey forth by "leaps."

One major "leap" apparently took place when they sailed southward with their Scythian partners into Afghanistan, Pakistan, Tibet, and northwestern India, where they became a rich, maritime people who were often referred to as white Hindus—children of the mother goddess Danu whose serpent children ruled the waters and settled in many lands. The serpent people are thought to have founded colonies "scattered all over southeast Asia, some regions of the South Pacific, Mexico, Central America and South America,"[4] carrying the Hindu religion with them. Thus, it is no surprise to note a connection between the old Vedic people of India and the early Maya of Mesoamerica.

As one author put it, the Danites were the pioneers of Israel. Although they and the Scythians and Celts merged with colonized regions throughout the world, they could be found in the greatest numbers along the west coast of Europe in Denmark (meaning Dan's Mark), and in Wales and England, Ireland, and Scandinavia.

2

America's Celtic Immigrants

The term *Celtic* refers to a group, or family, of languages primarily in Ireland, Scotland, Wales, Cornwall, the Isle of Man, and Brittany that have come to be known as the Six Celtic Nations. The Celtic languages form a branch of the larger Indo-European family from which Japheth's children descended.

Now, Japheth's descendants, with his son Gomer, initially settled throughout the Ukraine and lower Russia, where they were originally shepherds who descended from the Sacae, a warlike race of robbing and plundering people, some of which reached the colossal heights of eight and nine feet. A second group through Gomer's brother, Magog, are generally referred to as Scythians after the lands from which they came. The Scythians are described as a tall-statured, golden- or red-haired, fair-skinned, and blue-eyed race, although their pinkish skin often led to their being referred to as "red-skins." In Holinshed's *History of England*, we learn the children of Japheth inhabited Britain within two hundred years after the Great Flood. Others made it to the Iberian

Peninsula (Old Spain) about three hundred years after the Flood. E. Raymond Capt maintains that once they reached Portugal, the original colony divided, with one entering Ireland, and the other heading north into Denmark, Sweden, and Norway. However, the initial Celtic culture was formed by the Tuatha de Danann, meaning "the tribe of Dan," of Israelite origins. Moore's *History of Ireland* maintains that the "ancient Irish, called the 'Danai' or 'Danes,' separated from Israel around the time of the Exodus from Egypt, crossed to Greece and then invaded Ireland,"[1] with Gladstone adding that those who migrated from Greece to the Ireland became known as the Tuatha de Danann—the god-race of Ireland.

In Celtic mythology, the Tuatha de Danann were an ancient people skilled in magic who were banished from heaven because of their knowledge of the dark arts. They landed in a cloudy mist on the shores of ancient Ireland. While some believed they were a mythical race, it has now been proven that they were a genuine historical people, with the word *Tuatha* simply meaning "tribe"— they being of the tribe of Dan. While their leader, a man named Nuada, carried the blood of Israel through Dan, he was also linked by blood to the Scythians. It is said that Nuada's ancestral mother was the goddess Danu (a Danite mortal), while his paternal line went through Nemed, a descendant of Magog through Japheth. Thus, although carrying Israelite blood through his mother's line, Nuada was also a Scythian.

The Tuatha de Danann are described as the people of the goddess Danu, the goddess of darkness, and are credited with the formation of the Celtic society, whose priests spread out in all directions to teach the way of the gods to the people. Their mystic ways brought them into prominence in both historical records and books of mythology, in which giants roamed the land and wizards wielded powerful magic. But they are now considered a real people, a people described as energetic, progressive, skilled in metal work, and of having a superior knowledge of smelting and fabricating tools, weapons, and ornaments. In his *Book of Genealogies*, Dudley M. Firbis maintained that "everyone who is fair-haired, vengeful, large, and every plunderer, every musical person, the professor of musical and entertaining performances, who are adept in all Druidical and magical arts, they are the descendants of the Tuatha de Danann in Erin (Ireland)."

The Tuatha de Danann ruled Ireland for two hundred years until the Milesians invaded and took control of the island. While a variety of dates have been given for their arrival, *The Annals of Ireland* report that the Tuatha de Danann arrived in 1200 BC and ruled for two hundred years before being forced out by the Milesians. They left around 1000 BC, the very time Barry Fell concluded that Irish immigrants set sail in search of lands beyond the western skies. After studying the ancient scripts and Ogam-type writing found in various parts of America's New England states, Fell concluded that bands of roving Celtic mariners crossed the North Atlantic to colonize North America by way of the Canary Islands, the same route used by Columbus, which took him to the Caribbean. While he asserts that some initially settled in the West Indies, others who may not have been happy with the tropical climate after having lived so long in a temperate climate moved further northward and settled the rocky coasts and mountainous regions of New England, which was more like their own homeland—"there to establish a new European kingdom called *Iargalon*, 'land beyond the sunset.'"[2] Fell maintains that the Ogam letters found in Maine and Ireland are incontestably linked, and that the chances of the "17-letter Ogam alphabet of Monnegan, Maine, and Ireland" being of "independent origin in these two places are less than one in 300,000,000,000,000." In other words, zero![3]

Once settled, the Celts went on to build villages and temples and raise sacred circles, just as they had back in the Emerald Isle, with monuments raised to both the older Mother Goddess, and the pagan god Bel, or Baal. Their Druid priests instructed them in the worship of the sun, the moon, and the stars and their influence on their lives, their agricultural pursuits, and their prospects for their futures. The magic their shamans practiced was a form of Druidism that far surpasses the occult practices of today. Some suggest they even had power over death, an idea linked by some to the fountain of youth thought to be in either Florida or the Bimini Islands. So many Tuatha de Danann left the intolerable conditions imposed on them by the victorious Milesians that by the time of Christ, the Tuatha de Danann were all but extinct in Ireland, having transferred their magical ways to the "otherworld" of America.

No one knows where this band of Celts actually settled. However, there is a consensus that a number of waves of Celts arrived in America from various Celtic nations in the early centuries before Christ. Distinguished French architect M. Violet-le-duc maintains that a people referred to as Nahuas arrived from the north of Europe and settled in Florida, the West Indies, and up the Mississippi before descending upon Mexico.[4] The Nahuas were described as a highly civilized white race with an understanding of all the industrial arts, were gifted musicians and artists, and were just as familiar with magic and the dark arts as the Tuatha de Danaan.

Many of the Celts appeared to have arrived along the Atlantic coast on Phoenician ships whose merchant kings were intent on procuring copper from the Lake Superior copper mines, which contained the largest copper deposits in the world. The Old Copper Trade began mining large copper pits near Lake Superior around 3000 BC. They extracted copper and transported it down the

Mississippi River to the Gulf of Mexico, or out through the Great Lakes and the Saint Lawrence River to waiting ships along the Atlantic coast. While its destination is still unknown, it is believed that after being "refined in Wisconsin, Ireland and the Canary Islands, it was then transported to Egypt, the Mediterranean and Asia where it later fueled the Bronze Age."[5] Fell suggests that vast numbers of Celts were likely carried along on Phoenician ships to work the copper mines. Copper mining was a big business, and the more hands the better.

3

The Caribbean Empire & Prince Votan's Early Maya

A mighty seafaring man named Votan is said to have ruled a great Caribbean Empire anciently. Votan, a man considered the "great sun," or a "living god" to his subjects,[1] is said to have had seaports as far away as the Mediterranean and Norway, where his name was particular venerated, having come from a long line of Votans. Nineteenth century intellect Baron Von Humboldt claimed Votan was likely linked to the Scandinavian family of Wodan, who was a member of the same family as Odin of Celtic origin.[2]

In tracing the descent of Norwegian kings from the god

Odin the Wanderer
Georg von Rosen (1843–1923)

Odin, we find he was a real historical figure that some claim was of Danite/Scythian blood. He is said to have been a great conqueror and master wizard from the regions of the Black Sea who ultimately settled in the Scandinavian peninsula. He is described as a red-bearded, middle-aged man of enormous strength who was a force to be reckoned with against his enemies but was kind and benevolent to mankind—the description of a true Celtic god-hero.

Evidence that ancient Norsemen found their way to the northeast during the distant past was discovered on rock carvings found in Petersborough, southern Ontario.[3] After deciphering the carvings, Fell asserts that the engravings speak of an ancient Scandinavian voyage led by a Norwegian king named Woden-lithi, who arrived in 1700 BC. After establishing a permanent Norwegian settlement, and leaving a detailed inscription of his visit on a ninety-foot-long "crystalline marble outcrop," the king returned to Norway and was never heard from again.

The names *Votan*, *Odin*, and *Wodan*— especially Wodan—was known as far away as India where Celtic tribes congregated early in history. J. H. Baecker maintains that the three-, five-, seven-, and nine-headed snake is the totem of a race of rulers who presided over the Aryan, or white Hindus. This snake race,

A similar serpent ship

he observed, "was that of the first primeval seafarers," and that these "faring-wise serpent races became rulers and civilizers.[4]

One of Votan's most notable empires was established in the Caribbean waters, and it is believed one of his descendants went on to establish the early Maya Empire of Central America. Joseph Antonio Constantine believes Votan's grandfather arrived in the West Indies around 381 BC. Prince Votan III is thought to have been the last of the Caribbean sea-kings because the entire island empire was ultimately destroyed in some natural catastrophe. But until that fateful day, the island was a paradise, lavished with gold and jewels and embellished with copper and brass from the Lake Superior copper mines.

Tales of the great kingdom spread far and wide. Those in the old world were fascinated by the stories, and mariners were intent on finding it, not just for its treasures, but also as a place of refuge. After researching the thousands of books found in the Alexandria library for his own forty-volume *History of the World*, Diodorus of Sicily (80 BC) found evidence that the sea merchants of the Mediterranean were aware that such an island existed far across the ocean in the west as early as 400 BC.[5] After scholars ruled out England, and North or South America, it was concluded that one of the islands in the West Indies was most likely the island referred to.

Yet, strangely, the time came when no mention was ever made of the great western island again, which suggested to many that the greater island no longer existed and must have broken up into a number of smaller islands. The French historian Paul Gaffarel claimed that in 1892 the natives of the south Caribbean islands told Spanish chroniclers that the Antilles once formed a single continent, but was suddenly separated by the actions of the waters. Dr. Augustus Le Plongeon was one of the earliest to make this claim after translating the contents of the Troano manuscripts, which had several pages dedicated to the recital of "the awful phenomena that took place during the cataclysm that caused the submersion of ten countries."[6] The "indigenous people of the Caribbean Isles preserved the memory of a cataclysm and deluge which had separated the former land-mass into the thousands of islands and cays that make up the archipelagos we know today."[7]

A native who claimed to be a descendant of the last remaining grandson of the house of Votan to leave the island said that his illustrious ancestor, Prince Votan, had actually witnessed its destruction. The storyteller explained that the serpents at one time were the earth's sea-people, who with their mighty fleet of ships ruled the oceans and established colonies on many shorelines. But due to the many natural disasters that broke apart his island empire, the long history of the Votanic powers in the Gulf of Mexico was ended.

In telling the story, Sedillio, the war chief of the Yaqui, related that as the island's great volcano became more restless, Votan lined up his fleets in preparation for a quick departure. A tremendous cloud of black had spread over the heavens, and the earth had begun to shake. He maintains that it shook for days, then began to spurt fire like a great fountain as "the fire-god crawled through the caverns, roaring and thrashing the land about like a wolf shakes a rabbit."[8] There was no more time to waste. After placing the empire's books on board, along with "seeds for grain, food, drink, trees, animals, and their keep, as well as seeds for linen and cotton," the emperor gave his son Votan II instructions to head east, and his grandson Votan III instructions to head west.

The emperor continued to speak until the sacred mountain exploded, and everyone turned and fled for their lives. Votan's voice was deep as he tried to speak over the ever-increasing roar of the blast. He spoke, they say, like thunder with the aid of some small miracle that magnified his voice. Yet his voice was lost in the roar of the volcano and the screams of the people who stood in its hail of fire. Sedillio said: "We turned our dragons around and flew—many of them aflame."[9]

As the story of Votan continues, we learn that those fleeing the great destruction headed in all directions. Thus, cities began to rise all along the Gulf Coast and up the Mississippi, Illinois, and Ohio rivers where sub-suns began to rule various inland empires, with a particularly large ceremonial center built up at the cross of waters where the Mississippi meets the Missouri.

Legends claim Prince Votan III's company first made landfall in Massachusetts, where they celebrated a day of thanksgiving before making their way along the Gulf Coast to Mexico. Upon landing, Votan and his company moved inland and subsequently colonized and civilized parts of Chiapas and Guatemala. Traditions have Votan's father, Votan II, sailing back to Scandinavia where he was later worshiped as a god, while his uncle, a man named Tyr, is thought to have gone on to rule in the Tyrrhenian valley in the Mediterranean.[10] Nothing more is said of his grandfather, however. Thus, we must assume the emperor met his death in the fiery hail of the volcano along with many of the island's other residents.

Prince Votan III and his followers soon became the rulers of parts of the mainland and used their knowledge and organizational skills to unite the various tribal communities. It is said the locals submitted to his rule willingly and even offered up their daughters in their efforts to establish an alliance with them. Thus, the rise of one of the oldest cultures in Central America began— the early Maya. Yet, sadly, those who studied the Maya believe their religious ceremonies, which took place atop blood red temples like those formerly built on the isles, incorporated psychedelic drugs, bloodletting, phallic worship, and human sacrifice.

— 4 —

The Scattering of Israel

With Celtic mariners and refugees from Votan's drowned island paradise founding settlements along the Atlantic Coast and Florida, the new world was quickly filling up with sun-worshipers—the same pagan religion that caused the downfall of Israel. Sadly, much of the world had embraced the sun-worshiping religion introduced by Nimrod before the advent of Christianity. Those who have studied the subject maintain that the earliest form of sun-worship imbued the belief that the sun and the moon were alive and actually had human natures. Thus, the native populations of the early post-Flood world endowed them with a soul, a body, and parts and passions just like our own. Each nation that rose to power named their sun-god a different name, such as Osiris in Egypt, Baal or Moloch in Canaan, Bel in Babylon and Assyria, and Bacchus, Apollo, and Hercules in Rome. Actually, it was the power these gods sent forth to sustain the world that was worshiped, not the physical sun or moon itself.

In its earliest form, sun-worship was simply the worship of the principles of reproduction in both man and nature; then it was extended through all worship—the way the sun extends through all nature. The sun was regarded as the creator and the sustainer of all things. His wife, the moon, regulated the seasons and cycles of life. By whatever name the sun was worshiped, he was always associated with a female deity, because two were needed for reproduction. For example, Baal's wife was Ashtaroth, or Astare; Osiris had Isis; Adonis had Venus; and Apollo had Diana, with temples erected to both. Unfortunately, since the sun was the supreme lord of man and nature, whose most wondrous powers were reflected in the power to reproduce, prostitution was one of the chief characteristics of its worship wherever it was found. Therefore, the Lord was constantly stirred up against the Israelites because they chose such idolatrous forms of worship rather than worshipping him, even after all he had done for them.

Israel's fall from grace happened at the close of the eighth century BC. Not only was Israel constantly provoking the Lord to anger with their sun-worshiping ways, but it was also constantly instigating plots with neighboring tribes against Assyria, incurring their wrath as well. Thus, in 771 BC, the Assyrian king simply had had enough. He led his armies against Israel's northern kingdom, and thousands were subsequently killed or taken captive. The princes of Israel not taken in battle fled with their followers north toward the Caucasus Mountains; those left behind were forced to pay tribute and give service to their new masters. Without the means of mass communication, not much was heard of the tribes who disappeared. And it began to be noised about that *Israel was no more.*

Israel's two remaining tribes, Judah and Benjamin, and parts of Levi ruled the southern kingdom. They were relatively safe in Jerusalem during the time their kinsmen in the northern kingdom were being scattered to and fro. But the southern kingdom was destined to fall as well, because they had likewise taken up the worship of Baal—including its heinous practice of human sacrifice. Moreover, they burned incense in the high places, and on the hills and under every tree—acts forbidden by the Lord, who said:

> Thou shalt not plant thee a grove of any trees near unto the altar of the Lord thy God, which thou shalt make thee. Neither shalt thou set thee up any image; which the Lord thy God hateth. (Deuteronomy 16:21–22)

But, worse, they made molten images of Baalam, a pagan god, to whom they burned children just like the heathens did (see 2 Chronicles 28:1–4). The end for Israel's southern kingdom would soon follow in the path of the northern. Over and over the Lord warned his people not to indulge in such practices because they were an abomination in his sight. The Israelites were instructed to shun all types of sun-worship, and the Lord promised those who refused to obey that they would be cut off from among his people. So disgusted was the Lord with these pagan rituals that he said: "And the land is defiled: therefore I do visit the iniquity thereof upon it, and the land itself vomiteth out her inhabitants" (Leviticus 18:25).

In an effort to cleanse the land of this repugnant practice, the children of Israel were commanded to break down their images and destroy all their groves. Some were obedient to the Lord's command, but all through the period of the judges, there were repeated lapses back into sun-worshiping habits. During the reigns of Samuel and David, and in the early days of Solomon, they again

Moloch, sometimes called Ba'al Moloch, is known as the sacred Bull.

turned toward the Lord. But, in his later years, Solomon gave in to the demands of his wives, set up sacred groves again, and went after their false gods, such as Ashtaroth and the goddess Milcom of the Ammonites. He even went so far as to build a high place for Chemosh of the Moabites, and for Moleck of the children of Ammon, and burnt incense and sacrificed to their gods, (see 1 Kings 11:1–8). Ahab followed the god of Baal after marrying Jezebel, and he built up more altars and places of worship for this heathen god. Tragically, in time there were more worshipers of Baal than there were of Jehovah.

Elijah did much to eradicate sun-worship from the land, yet by Manasseh's time, the tradition had returned, and once again high places were built, altars were reared for Baal, and groves were planted for all the hosts of heaven. To make matters worse, he erected altars in the temple of the Lord and caused children to be passed through the fire in the valley of Hinnom.

> And he caused his children to pass through the fire in the valley of the son of Hinnom: also he observed times, and used enchantments, and used witchcraft, and dealt with a familiar spirit, and with wizards: he wrought much evil in the sight of the Lord, to provoke him to anger. (2 Chronicles 33:6)

Magic and witchcraft had also crept into the land. Manasseh even placed a carved image in the temple of Solomon, where the Lord had said: "In this house and in Jerusalem, . . . will I put my name forever."

Thankfully, Josiah, who succeeded Manasseh, annihilated the whole system of sun-worship again, including its high places and groves. However, by Zedekiah's reign, sun-worship was back, but even worse, it had evolved into the worship of the sun itself, with the priests turning their backs on the temple to worship that luminary—a form of apostasy.

The Lord could bear it no longer, withdrew his Spirit, and allowed Nebuchadnezzar to bring a large army against Jerusalem. He took the city, sacked the temple, and killed or captured the choicest sons of Judah, leaving only the peasant stock behind. The scattering of the southern kingdom of Judah also began. While historians claim that all of King Zedekiah's sons were killed, the Book of Mormon reveals that one son was spared and made his way to the promised land, as did Lehi and his colony, whose story comes next.

Part Two

The Land of Promise

∼ 5 ∼

Lehi's Land of Promise

The arrival of the Nephites into the land of promise brought Israel's first immigrants into a land blessed above all others, a land near New York's Hill Cumorah. They spread out in all directions over the centuries, only to fall as a nation nine hundred years later in consequence of sin—only the Lamanites remained.

According to the Prophet Joseph Smith, the bones of the lost Mound Builders of the northeast are Nephites. While traveling west with the men of Zion's Camp, he wrote:

> We arrived this morning on the banks of the Mississippi, . . . we left the eastern part of the state of Ohio. . . . The whole of our journey . . . wandering over the plains of the Nephites, recounting occasionally the history of the Book of Mormon, roving over the mounds of that once beloved people of the Lord, picking up their skulls & their bones, as proof of its divine authenticity, and gazing upon a country the fertility, the splendor and the goodness so indescribable.[1]

As to their distant origins, in the *Teachings of the Prophet Joseph*

Smith, we learn the Prophet Joseph tied the American Indians to that Joseph who was sold into Egypt. He claimed that the land of America is a promised land to the American Indians. As far back as Jaredite times, the Lord revealed to the prophet Ether that Jerusalem would fall and that a remnant of the seed of Joseph would be led out of the land to preserve them from destruction.

He said:

> Wherefore, the Lord brought a remnant of the seed of Joseph out of the land of Jerusalem, that he might be merciful unto the seed of Joseph that they should perish not, even as he was merciful unto the father of Joseph that he should perish not.
>
> Wherefore, the remnant of the house of Joseph shall be built upon this land; and it shall be a land of their inheritance; and they shall build up a holy city unto the Lord, like unto the Jerusalem of old; and they shall no more be confounded, until the end come when the earth shall pass away. (Ether 13:7–8)

Bruce R. McConkie reaffirms that Joseph's land of inheritance was America in a talk explaining the gathering of Israel in the last days. He said, "The house of Joseph will be established in America, the house of Judah in Palestine, and that the Lost Tribes will come to Ephraim in America to receive their blessings in due course."[2]

Lehi speaks of the promised land in 2 Nephi, mentioning that it will be the land of inheritance for his seed.

> Notwithstanding our afflictions, we have obtained a land of promise, a land which is choice above all other lands; a land which the Lord God hath covenanted with me should be a land for the inheritance of my seed. Yea, the Lord hath covenanted this land unto me, and to my children forever, and also all those who should be led out of other countries by the hand of the Lord (2 Nephi 1:5).

The law of Moses

Several clues help us identify North America as the covenant lands of Joseph and the land of inheritance of Lehi's seed. For instance, we must remember that the Nephites were Israelites and had to be led to a land with a temperate climate. The law of Moses includes the seasonal cycles of the moon, with the observance of Passover, Pentecost, and Sukkoth following the harvests of certain grains in the spring, summer, and fall, such as wheat, corn, and barley.

Another important clue is found in Ether 13:2–3, which says that the New Jerusalem will be built in the promised land. Further light on the location of the New Jerusalem is found in Doctrine and Covenants 124:51, which reveals that the city of Zion will be built in Jackson County, Missouri, in what is now the United States of America. It was in the land of promise the Father and the Son appeared to Joseph Smith and also where the angel Moroni came to Joseph and gave him charge over the sacred gold plates. And it will be on this choice land that Christ will reign as King of Kings and Lord of Lords, over the earth during his glorious millennial reign.

Another clue of major importance is found in the Book of Mormon where we learn that the promised land was set apart to be a land of liberty to those who worship Christ. We read in Ether:

> Behold, this is a choice land, and whatsoever nation shall possess it shall be free from bondage, and from captivity, and from all other nations under heaven, if they will but serve the God of the land, who is Jesus Christ. (Ether 2:12)

New Jerusalem

America was liberated from the grasp of all other nations during the Revolutionary War. As tragic as that war was, it set the stage for the founding of a new republic. Nephi was actually allowed to see that war in vision, which he then recorded as follows:

> I, Nephi, beheld that the Gentiles . . . had gone forth out of captivity. . . . And I beheld that their mother Gentiles were gathered together upon the waters . . . to battle against them. . . And I, Nephi, beheld that the Gentiles that had gone out of captivity were delivered by the power of God out of the hands of all other nations. (1 Nephi: 13:16–19)

President Ezra Taft Benson spoke of that important point in history. He said:

> God revealed over twenty-five hundred years ago that the kingdoms of Europe would try to exercise dominion over the colonists who had fled to America, that this would lead to a struggle for independence, and that the colonists would win. The Book of Mormon foretold the time when the colonists

would establish this as a land of liberty which would not be governed by kings. The Lord declared that He would protect the land and whoever would attempt to establish kings from within or without would perish.[3]

On another occasion, President Benson explained just how important that war actually was, because it set the stage for the founding of our modern form of government and the Restoration and coming forth of the Book of Mormon. He said:

Our Father in Heaven planned the coming forth of the Founding Fathers and their form of government as the necessary great prologue leading to the restoration of the gospel. Recall what our Savior said nearly two thousand years ago when he visited this promised land; for . . . it is wisdom in the Father that they should be established in this land, and be set up as a free people by the power of the Father, that these things might come forth.[4]

In the Saturday morning session of general conference on October 4, 1975, Marion G. Romney said of America: "This is a choice land, and whatsoever nation shall possess it shall be free from bondage, and from captivity, and from all other nations under heaven, if they will but serve the God of the land, who is Jesus Christ (2 Nephi 1:6–7)." He then went on to speak of the ancient inhabitants of America:

In the western part of the state of New York near Palmyra is a prominent hill known as the hill Cumorah. On July twenty-fifth of this year, as I stood on the crest of that hill admiring with awe the breathtaking panorama which stretched out before me on every hand, my mind reverted to the events which occurred in that vicinity some twenty-five centuries ago—events which brought an end to the great Jaredite nation. And why were they exterminated? Because they forgot the Lord's everlasting decree that only those nations who worshiped Him would prosper in the promised land, and that all others would be wiped away, and so they were . . . the tragic fate of the Jaredite and the Nephite civilizations is proof positive that the Lord meant it when he said that: "this a land of promise; and whatsoever nation shall possess it shall serve God, or they shall be swept off when the fulness of his wrath shall come upon them. And the fulness of his wrath cometh upon them when they are ripened in iniquity" (Ether 2:9).

Both the Jaredites and Nephites learned just how serious the Lord was about that matter. The next in line to inherit the promised land were the Gentiles. Thus, when the time was right, the

The first Thanksgiving at Plymouth

Lord inspired Christian men and women to leave the Old World and head for America, where they could live their religion in peace. They initially came in small groups, then in shiploads, all looking to escape persecution of one kind or another and to have the liberty and freedom to worship as they pleased. Although they were of many faiths, they all worshipped Jesus Christ.

Dutch Puritans were just as eager to find relief from struggles and religious oppression. In time a steady stream of people sailed from the Netherlands across the Atlantic to America, most of whom carried a preponderance of Israelite blood. Some came to find religious freedom, others came in hopes of finding wealth, and some came to convert the American Indians to the religion of Christ and to plant a new commonwealth in the New World. Thus, it was with a strong hope of a new beginning that the Puritans of Holland left their own garden-like land to make a new life in the New World where they found a new garden spot to cultivate. The soil was fertile and rich with timber, and numerous waterways cut through the land, providing trade routes in all directions. The Dutch planted the

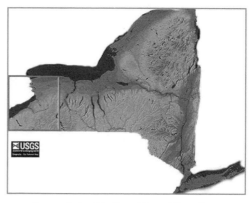

Area of the Holland Land Purchase

first seeds of civilization on the soil of what would later become five of the thirteen colonies: New York, New Jersey, Connecticut, Pennsylvania, and Delaware.

In 1792, the Dutch purchased 3,250,000 acres of land between Lake Erie and the Genesee River, stretching from Lake Ontario on the north to the Pennsylvania line on the south. The purchase came to be known as the Holland Land Purchase—a territory that matches in every way the heartland of Book of Mormon territory. In fact, the borders of the territory purchased by the Dutch outlines almost exactly the three principal lands described in the Book of Mormon.

6

The Arrival
of the Nephites

The Dutch came to America by way of the Canary Islands rather than across the north Atlantic. Following currents northward, they ultimately sailed up the Hudson River to New York. They set up some of their northern outposts along the old Iroquois trail, a narrow path beaten down by American Indian feet over the centuries and which led from the Mohawk River clear to Niagara. Letters sent home to Holland claimed the colonists never wanted to return, for whatever paradise they had in Holland, the same bounties could be found in their new surroundings. These letters enticed even more of the oppressed in the Netherlands to brave the Atlantic to join them.

The Atlantic was no doubt the route used by the Nephites to come to America as well. A lot was going on in the years before the Babylonian invasion of Jerusalem and the fall of Israel's Southern Kingdom. The northern tribes had already been scattered, and prophets were prophesying about the destruction of Jerusalem if the southern tribes did not repent because they were worshiping the

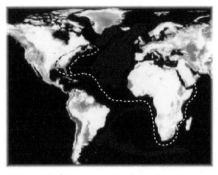

Lehi's route to America

pagan god Baal. Lehi was among those crying repentance; he loved his people and his homeland and could not bear the thought of their destruction. So he knelt in prayer and prayed with all his heart in behalf of his people, which left him totally exhausted. After returning home, he fell on his bed and was carried away in vision in which he saw the destruction of Jerusalem.

After such a sobering experience, Lehi valiantly went out among his countrymen again and implored them to return to the Lord's ways lest their city be destroyed. Rather than repent, however, the people mocked Lehi, cast stones at him, and sought to take away his life. Thus, the Lord spoke to him in a dream, instructing him to take his family and flee into the wilderness with the promise that they would be led to a land choice above all others (see 1 Nephi 2:1–2).

Along with his wife and daughters, his four sons, Laman, Lemuel, Sam, and Nephi, accompanied Lehi into the unknown. For the most part, his family was supportive—except his two oldest sons, Laman and Lemuel, who caused trouble from the journey's beginning and continued their rebellious attitudes throughout the trip to the promised land, and long after.

With not-so-friendly nations in control of the Mediterranean ports, it appears the Lord had Lehi's family detour into the Arabian desert and then eastward to the Arabian Sea. The scriptures give no indication of what route the Nephites followed once they set sail, but since they ended up in the regions around Cumorah in New York State, we can suppose they sailed west

Lehi's route inland

and rounded the southern tip of Africa into the Atlantic Ocean. After some three thousand miles, natural ocean currents hook to the northwest and then westward to South America, and they would have picked up the North Equatorial Current. Farther north, the currents move along the Atlantic coast clear to the Saint Lawrence River, which leads inland right to New York. But it appears the Lord led the Nephites inland along a southern route—perhaps from Chesapeake Bay along the west branch of the Susquehanna, which would have led with a short portage to the Alleghey River that heads in southwestern New York or from the gulf waters up the Mississippi River to the Ohio and then east to the Allegheny—the Lord led Mulek into the lands to the north, and Lehi into the land south (see Helaman 6:10).

If ascending the Mississippi, they likely diverted into the Ohio

Mississippi River

Ohio River

River, which runs along the periphery of both a humid subtropical climate and a humid continental climate that helped foster the growth of plants and animals indigenous to both regions. Turning north, the Ohio River diverts into the Allegheny River, once considered part of the Ohio. The river continues northward, much of it flowing through hilly woodlands. Thus, the Lord likely directed Lehi's company into the old Venago branch of the river, now called French Creek, although it is still generally considered a river. French Creek is one of the most biologically diverse streams east of the Mississippi River, providing habitat to over eighty species of fish and twenty-six species of freshwater mussel. Considering its bounties, the Nephites may have initially settled along the river before moving into southwestern New York, which became the land of their first inheritance.

While the tropics have a more genial climate, the Nephites knew they needed to settle a region that had four distinct seasons so they could comply with all of the ordinances of the law of Moses.

Allegheny River

Upper Allegheny River

As the Hebrew scholar Vincent Coon points out, certain priesthood ordinances relevant to the law of Moses needed to be in sync with Jerusalem's seasons, which could only happen in the northern hemisphere.

Lehi landing in America

As time passed, Nephi and his younger brother Jacob proved to be righteous men, and they provided some of the most profound doctrine and spiritual insights found in any recorded scripture. But their brothers Laman and Lemuel were not so noble. In fact, they continually sought to take Nephi's life. So the followers of Nephi moved a little further north where they settled a second region that they called the land of Nephi, after Nephi, which was the custom of the time.

Part Three

Outlining Book of Mormon Territory

Defining Borders, Lands, and Seas

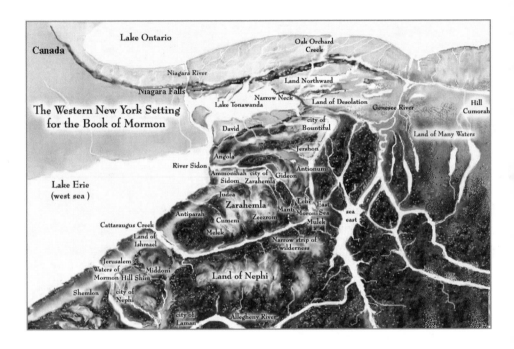

The Western New York Setting for the Book of Mormon

Lake Ontario

Canada

Oak Orchard Creek

Niagara River

Land Northward

Niagara Falls

Narrow Neck

Lake Tonawanda

Land of Desolation

Genesee River

Hill Cumorah

city of Bountiful

David

Land of Many Waters

Jershon

Angola

River Sidon

Antionum

Ammonihah city of Gideon
Sidom Zarahemla

Lake Erie
(west sea)

Judea

Zarahemla

Lehi East
Manti Moroni Sea
Mulek

sea
east

Antiparah

Cumeni

Zeezrom

Cattaraugus Creek

Melek

Land of
Ishmael

Narrow strip of
wilderness

Jerusalem

Waters of
Mormon Hill Shim

Middoni

Land of Nephi

Shemlon

city of
Nephi

city of
Laman

Allegheny River

~ 7 ~

Defining Book of Mormon Territory

Several topographical features and cultural traits noted in the scriptures must be reconciled in any search for Book of Mormon territory, including the following:

1—The land south descended in elevation from south to north.

2—A narrow strip of wilderness separated the Nephites and Lamanites.

3—Seas were on both the east and the west of the land of Nephi.

4—The soil and climate were suitable for agriculture.

5—The lands of Nephi and Zarahemla were nearly surrounded by water.

6—The head of the north-flowing river Sidon was in the southeastern corner of the land.

7—The Nephites built fortifications throughout the land.

8—Bountiful was described as being only 1½ day's journey wide.

9—A line of some kind also separated Bountiful from Desolation.

10—The land northward included a sea that divided the land.

11—A narrow neck of land passed through its waters.

12—Both heat and cold were noted in the scriptures.

13—There were serpents in the land, and also fevers.

14—Elephants once roamed the land.

15—A seashore of some kind existed to the east of the Hill Cumorah

16—The hill Cumorah was in a land of many waters, rivers and fountains.

17—Large bodies of water were nearby.

18—Gold, silver, copper, and other minerals in the area.

19—They had a written language.

20—The land of Cumorah was the scene of major warfare.

The Topography of the Land

The territory along the far western borders of New York matches the description of the Nephite's land southward amazingly well: a land that descended in elevation the farther north one travels. Because of the northward slope of the land, the rivers in the area flowed north, just as the Sidon does in the scriptures. The Nephites traveling north always referred

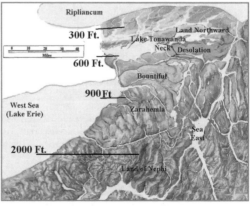

Topography of the land

it as traveling down, while those traveling south described it as traveling up. In the New York setting, the land of Nephi is filled with hills and valleys, with gently rolling hills more prevalent in Zarahemla and plains filling the territory further north toward Bountiful.

The Seas to the East and the West

It is important to know that the Hebrews called their lakes "seas." But because so many lakes existed in Book of Mormon territory, it would have been confusing to name them like they did the sea of Galilee. So Book of Mormon scribes simply described them in relation to their position in the land, such as they did in Alma 22: 27, which simply described Lamanite territory as "bordering even to the sea, on the east and on the west."

While the sea on the west can easily be reconciled with Lake Erie, the sea on the east is not as readily recognized in the modern setting. Yet by searching the geological record, we find that an ancient sea actually did exist in the southern course of the Genesee River at one time—a remnant of the last ice age that left "the

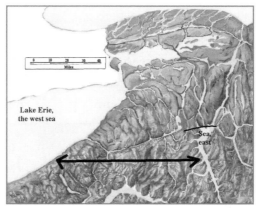

A morainal dam blocked the path of the Genesee anciently, which allowed a lake (or sea) to form.

greatest series of ice-impounded waters [across New York] ever produced."[1] Most of the lakes ultimately drained away. However, Herbert LeRoy Fairchild, the foremost authority on the Genesee River, maintains that a morainal dam in the broad valley along the southern course of the river forced the river waters into its tributary valleys, especially those in the west, which allowed an ancient lake to form. Fairchild stated that the evidence of standing waters in this area is clear and conspicuous, having been recorded by the wave action of the lake along its shores, and the deltas it formed.[2] He believed the lake must have remained in the area for a considerable period, for it had to first cut through 75 feet of drift and then 125 feet of portage shale before it could drain northward again. Once the waters broke through, they ran through a narrow gorge with such force that they ultimately carved out a spectacular canyon called the "Grand Canyon of the East," today. While the northern course of the river could no longer be considered a sea, the lake held in the broad valley to the south matches the description of a sea to the east of Lamanite territory very well.

The Narrow Strip of Wilderness that Separated the Lands of Nephi and Zarahemla

Whatever bounties the Nephites found in the lands they first colonized, the Lamanites were such a threat that the Lord led the Nephites through the wilderness and into the land of Zarahemla, where a natural line of demarcation separated the two people. It seems the territory between Lake Erie and the Genesee River is divided in half by an east-west trending waterway, which cuts across the land for a distance of sixty-eight miles. Alma explains:

> And it came to pass that the king sent a proclamation throughout all the land, . . . in all the regions round about . . . which was divided from the land of Zarahemla by a narrow strip of wilderness, which ran from the sea east even to the sea west, and round about on the borders of the seashore, and the borders of the wilderness which was on the north by the land of Zarahemla, through the borders of Manti, by the head of the river Sidon, running from the east towards the west—and thus were the Lamanites and the Nephites divided. (Alma 22:27)

Note that two different wildernesses were being described in Alma 22:27: one that extended from the sea east to the sea west, and a second in the north by the land of Zarahemla, which extended from the head of the River Sidon westward. While one wilderness would have sufficed as a border, the inclusion of two would presuppose something lay between, such as western New York's Cattaraugus Creek, which carries the

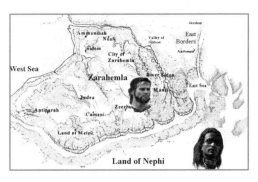

51

Cattauraugus Creek
Courtesy Floyd James

water sixty-eight miles from its head westward to Lake Erie, form-
ing a natural line of demarcation between two regions. While not
an insurmountable barrier, the line between the Nephites and
Lamanites was no small thing. Cattaraugus Creek is over three
hundred feet across in places and swift enough to attract people
from all over the country who enjoy whitewater rafting and
kayaking.

Interestingly, archaeologists noted a definite difference between
the ancient fortifications found to the south of this line and those
to the north. While they agreed that they were all defensive in
nature, the differences in their construction led them to believe
the creek formed a line of demarcation between two opposing
cultural groups. How right they were without even knowing the
differences between the Nephites and Lamanites.

Despite their relative safety in Zarahemla, some Nephites
wanted to reclaim the lands of their first inheritance. Therefore, a
few, under the leadership of a man named Zeniff, ventured back

into the land of Nephi hoping to acquire permission to rebuild and settle in one of their old cities. Not only was this a bad lapse in judgment but also a huge mistake. The Lamanites saw this as an opportunity to place the Nephite settlers in bondage and glut themselves with the bounties they produced because the Lamanites were a lazy people. Once permission was granted, the people of Zeniff immediately began to renovate the city and plant crops, and just as the Lamanites planned, the Nephites were soon placed in bondage.

The rolling hills and great variety of soil in this region, particularly in Chautauqua County, contains some of the leading agricultural regions of New York. The belt along Lake Erie's shores is lower in altitude and warmer, providing for a delayed autumn and nearly frost-free spring, making it possible for fruits and grains, which normally require a more temperate climate, to flourish in the area.

Grapes

In 1920 there were 35,000 acres of vineyards, some perhaps grown from stock planted by King Noah during the Nephite era.

> And it came to pass that he [King Noah] planted vineyards round about in the land; and he built winepresses, and made wine in abundance; and therefore he became a winebibber, and also his people. (Mosiah 11:15)

Other crops also thrived during the Nephite era, many that are grown in the Chautauqua County today.

> And we began to till the ground, yea, even with all manner of seeds, with seeds of corn, and of wheat, and of barley, and with neas, and with sheum, and with seeds of all manner of

fruits; and we did begin to multiply and prosper in the land (Mosiah 9:9).

William A. Ritchie states that the weather began to trend toward cooler and moister conditions during the Woodlands time period (1000–600 BC), although it still remained somewhat warmer until around the time of Christ when a cool, moist climate prevailed.[3]

8

The Land of Zarahemla

Moving north from the land of Nephi puts us in Erie County, which has hill country to the south and gently rolling hills and plains further north. Much of the area was forested before the Dutch cleared the land and planted their crops. We can suppose the Mulekites did the same thing when they first entered the land, for the Jaredites kept the land southward as a hunting preserve and had not disturbed it.

In the area, most of the archaeological remains of the ancient occupants have been found in the central section along Buffalo Creek, which runs through the heart

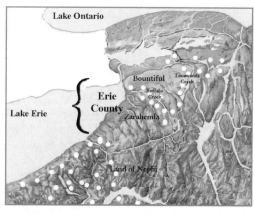

Erie County, the proposed land of Zarahemla

Buffalo Harbor in 1825

of the land, and along Tonawanda Creek, which forms the east borders of Erie county, the likely east borders of Nephite territory as well.

The fertile soil in Erie County made agriculture the leading industry for Dutch settlers once they settled the land. The waters off Lake Erie modify the climate, which is particularly advantageous in growing fruit. However, grains were their main crop. In 1850, for instance, 3.25 million bushels of wheat were exported. In 1860, 18.5 bushels of wheat were exported, and corn exported in the amount of 7.3 bushels. So much grain was shipped that by 1825 Buffalo Harbor was considered the greatest storehouse of grain in the world.

The Buffalo River is a creek for most of its course, starting at its headwaters in the far southeast corner of Erie County. It winds northward through the land in a zigzag pattern, then westward where it becomes a full-fledged river before emptying into Lake Erie (most likely the west sea noted in the Book of Mormon). Many relics and ancient fortifications found in Erie County have been found along Buffalo Creek, and some are consistent with the people and timeline for the Nephites, a topic that will be addressed later. By following the movements of

Buffalo Creek today

Buffalo Creek today
Photo courtesy Buffalo/Niagara RIVERKEEPERS

the Nephites and the many journeys described in the Book of Mormon, it becomes obvious that the Sidon followed the natural northward slope of the land, flowing north and out to sea, just as Buffalo Creek does today—the two probably being the same waterway. Even though it is a creek for most of its course, the Nephites would likely have describe it as a *brook*. In Hebrew, the word *nachal* is used to describe both a river and a brook and thus would rightly describe both Buffalo River and its beginnings as Buffalo Creek.

There can be little doubt that Buffalo Creek carried much more water anciently than it does today, for there is consensus that the rivers and creeks in the area were deeper before the time of European colonization than they are today. Even so, the Sidon was still shallow enough that the armies of the Nephites and Lamanites were able to cross it to battle one another whenever the need arose. During one altercation with the Lamanites and Amlicites, for instance, the Lamanites fell upon the Nephites

Buffalo Creek
Courtesy Buffalo/Niagra RIVERKEEPERS

Buffalo Creek
Courtesy Floyd James

while they were crossing the Sidon. So terrible was that battle that the Nephites had to clear the ground on the west side of the river to make room for those on the other side to join the battle.

> And thus he cleared the ground, or rather the bank, which was on the west of the river Sidon, throwing the bodies of the Lamanites who had been slain into the waters of Sidon, that thereby his people might have room to cross and contend with the Lamanites and the Amlicites on the west side of the river Sidon. (Alma 2:34)

Interestingly, the Hebrew word for *Sidon,* or *tsidon,* means fishing or fishery. Three ancient sites (called the Sinking Ponds Wildlife Sanctuary) along the ancient course of the river have been identified as fisheries. Perhaps these sites are another reason the river was called Sidon.

Sinking Ponds Wildlife Sanctuary
Courtesy Vincent Coon

Other sites in the Sinking Ponds Wildlife Sanctuary date back to Jaredite times. Perhaps Lib in the Book of Mormon frequented the area.

And in the days of Lib the poisonous serpents were destroyed. Wherefore they did go into the land southward, to hunt food . . . for the land was covered with animals of the forest. And Lib also himself became a great hunter. (Ether 10:19)

A view of the rolling hills of modern Erie County
Courtesy Vincent Coon

Western New York's Erie County is a beautiful land. There can be little doubt that it was beautiful back in Nephite times as well, with dwellings dotting the landscape just as they do today.

Timberlands

The forests in the surrounding hill country had ample timber for the Nephites to construct their villages and towns. "And I did teach my people to build buildings, and to work in all manner of wood" (2 Nephi 5:15). During colonial times, western New York was considered the greatest lumber place in the world. So it is no surprise to learn the Nephites and Jaredites built their cities with wood, all of which were burned to the ground at the end of their respective eras. The descending Iroquois tribes may have learned their house-building skills from their ancient Nephite fathers.

The only thing that survived the Lamanites' burning frenzy was the

Forest

Iroquois Longhouse
Courtesy Vincent Coon

post holes used in constructing their homes. Even less was discovered in Jaredite sites.

Jaredite Era— Now the name of the brother of Lib was called Shiz. And it came to pass that Shiz pursued after Coriantumr, and he did overthrow many cities, and he did slay both women and children, and *he did burn the cities*. (Ether 14:17; emphasis added)

Nephite Era—And it came to pass that whatsoever lands we had passed by, and the inhabitants thereof were not gathered in, were destroyed by the Lamanites, *and their towns, and villages, and cities were burned with fire*; and thus three hundred and seventy and nine years passed away. (Mormon 5:5; emphasis added)

Even their temples were constructed with wood. King Noah embellished the temple with fine wood in his day.

And he also caused that his workmen should work all manner of fine work within the walls of the temple, *of fine wood*, and of copper, and of brass. (Mosiah 11:10; emphasis added)

Actually, the Lord forbade the Israelites from building their altars in hewn stone. In Exodus, 20:25–26, we read: "And if thou wilt make me an altar of stone, thou shalt not build it of hewn stone: for if thou lift up thy tool upon it, thou hast polluted it.

Neither shalt thou go up by steps unto mine altar, that thy nakedness be not discovered thereon.@

Hugh Nibley said:

In view of the nature of their civilizations one should not be puzzled if the Nephites had left us no ruins at all. People underestimate the capacity of things to disappear, and do not realize that the ancients almost never built of stone. Many a great civilization which has left a notable mark in history and in literature has left behind not a single recognizable trace of itself. We must stop looking for the wrong things. [1]

Nephite Fortifications

While almost all evidence of the Nephite civilization has been lost to us, remnants of their sturdy fortifications have been found across the land, including Buffalo Creek. A number of Iroquois leaders have also been buried there. A large Indian cemetery at Buffalo contains the bones of Red Jacket who E. G. Squire describes as the "last and noblest of the proud and polite Iroquois . . . who died exulting that the Great Spirit had made him an Indian."[2]

Squire describes a fort on the edge of a second terrace of Buffalo Creek that was elevated above the fertile alluviums bordering the creek. He went on to explain that the enclosure had a trench and embankment with the wall crowned with pickets, just like those noted in Alma 50:2–5. Generations of Iroquois still revere a nearby mound that covered the victims of a conflict in "olden times."[3]

These Iroquois villages and cities were fortified with high walls of timber, a custom the Lamanites perpetuated throughout the ages. Their

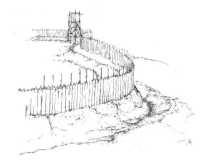

Illustration of fort and ditch by John Olive

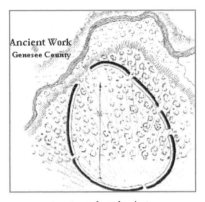

Ancient fortified site

customs of encircling their cities with timber was likely learned from their ancient fathers, who also built circular or elliptical villages judging by their post holes. Even the city of Bountiful may have been circular judging by the following scripture.

And he caused that they should build a breastwork of timbers upon the inner bank of the ditch; and they cast up dirt out of the ditch against the breastwork of timbers; and thus they did cause the Lamanites to labor until they had *encircled* the city of Bountiful *round about* with a strong wall of timbers and earth, to an exceeding height. (Alma 53:4; emphasis added)

An elliptical Iroquois village
Courtesy Vincent Coon

Bountiful and the East Borders

Moving north from Zarahemla takes us into Bountiful, the northernmost territory in the land southward. When the Dutch settled near Lake Erie and cleared the land of its timber, they found a soil as fertile as any in the state. During the early years of colonization, agriculture flourished in this region. Dr. James Sullivan maintains that anything that did well in a temperate climate does well in this area.

The city of Bountiful likely lay near the modern city of Batavia, where the northward flowing Tonawanda Creek (called a river in the eighteenth century) cascades over the Onondaga

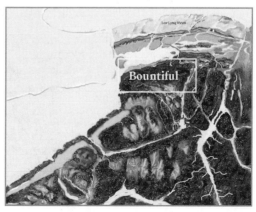

The territory of Bountiful

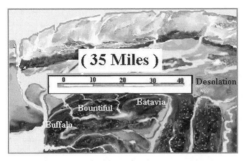

The distance from Lake Erie to Batavia

escarpment and onto the plains below. The distance from Lake Erie to Batavia is thirty-five miles—the very distance a Nephite could walk in a day and a half, just as described in Alma 22:32. "And now, it was only the distance of *a day and a half's journey* for a Nephite, on the line Bountiful and the land Desolation, from the east to the west sea." An old Indian trail along the limestone cliffs of the Onondaga escarpment bordering Bountiful on the north may be "*the line Bountiful*" mentioned in this scripture. As late as 1804, Joseph Ellicott, chief surveyor for agents intent on purchasing lands in the area, claimed to have followed an old Indian path along the crest of the escarpment from Batavia to Buffalo River for most of that distance.

Archaeological evidence indicates that the favorable location around Batavia was inhabited as far back as Jaredite times, and it may even have been the site of the ancient city of Moron. In more modern times, it is considered the birthplace of western New York, because all roads led to and from Batavia once the Dutch moved into the area. Its position at the crossroads of the land southward and northward also made it a favorable location for the city of Bountiful, a place that ultimately became holy ground when the Savior visited the Nephites in Bountiful

Tonawanda Creek

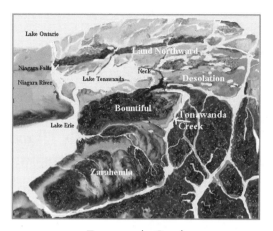

Tonawanda Creek

following his death and resurrection.

Interestingly, the bend where the river Tonawanda turns west at Batavia is sometimes called de-o-on-go-wa, or the *Great Hearing Place,* by the Indians. Could this be in reference to the time their ancient fathers heard the words of the Master, who arrived in Bountiful among the faithful to preach the everlasting gospel?

A long, fingerlike glacial lake once existed in the valley that carries Tonawanda Creek northward today. The lake was fed primarily by headwaters that originated in the valley to the south of it, which also held a glacial lake anciently. In fact the glacial waters in the area fed three major waterways: Buffalo Creek, Cattaraugus Creek, and Tonawanda Creek. Not surprisingly, the ancient lake the Nephites called the east sea lay just to the east of the head of the river Sidon's head. Thus, the two bodies of water are probably the same.

A belt of morainal dams held the lake captive for a time, forcing it to find outlets wherever it could. Once it found these areas of discharge, the lake drained in three different directions: one north into Tonawanda Creek (which formed the Nephite's eastern borders),

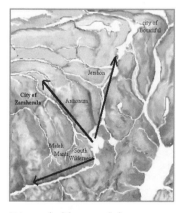

Waters held around the east sea discharged in three directions.

one northwest into Buffalo Creek (which formed the eastern and northern borders of Zarahemla), and one southwest into Cattaraugus Creek (which formed the line between the Nephites and Lamanites).

The watershed area that feeds these creeks receives an average annual rainfall of forty-four inches, and ample winter snows replenish the swamps and small kettle lakes that still fill the area today. The only remaining lake of any significance is Java Lake, which continues to feeds Cattaraugus Creek. The swamps of Beaver Meadows still feed Buffalo Creek, and Gallagher Swamps and Faun Lake still feed Tonawanda Creek.

During Nephite times, the east borders must have been an inviting place to live, for the scriptures indicate that a number of Nephite cities existed along the east sea. While the swift waters of Cattaraugus Creek formed a line of demarcation between Nephite and Lamanite territory, they were apparently not too great an obstacle to cross, for the Lamanites made every effort to take control of the cities along the east borders, including the cities of Moroni, Lehi, Morianton, Omner, Gid, and Mulek. However, we would have to place the city of Mulek somewhere along the southern edge of the sea which extended somewhat into Lamanite territory, for the scriptures refer Mulek as the strongest stronghold of the Lamanites in the land of Nephi (see Alma 53:6).

While the close proximity of the east sea to Lamanite territory made this area vulnerable to attack, it was also vulnerable to earthquakes for the Clarendon/Linden Fault runs right alongside Tonawanda Creek. Most

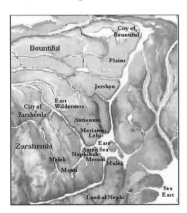

Eastern borders

earthquake activity along the fault hits Attica, a city about midway along the creek. In 1929, an earthquake hit Attica, registering only 5.6 on the Richter scale, but the waters in the area overflowed their basins, wells went dry, chimneys were toppled, walls cracked, and people ran from their homes in panic. As insignificant as it was compared to the one that hit the area at the time of the Savior's death, the Attica earthquake of 1929 was felt over one hundred thousand square miles. In 1944, another earthquake centered on the New York/Canadian line was felt from the Atlantic to the Mississippi, and from Canada to South Carolina. Think of the devastation that must have hit at the time of the Savior's Crucifixion. The scriptures state that the entire city of Moroni, built by the east sea, sank into the waters and its inhabitants drowned (3 Nephi 8:9).

Because of their vulnerability to attack, all the cities along the east borders were fortified—from the east sea northward all the way to the city of Bountiful, where the modern city of Batavia lies. The report of a nineteenth-century survey done by E. G. Squire noted the discovery of a double fortified fort near Batavia. Not more than six miles away, the remnant of an entire town was discovered, which included two forts. The first fort contained four acres, with the other about two miles away enclos-

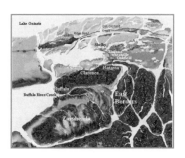

Batavia and forts

ing eight acres. The ditch around the town measured six feet, with a stream and a high bank encircling nearly a third of the enclosed ground. A funeral pyre was found near the western fort "where the slain had been buried after a great battle."[1]

A number of fortifications were also found on the northern borders of Bountiful along the Onondaga escarpment. The forts were

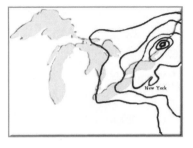

Earthquake activity

about a mile or two apart in areas where large natural openings occurred in the ancient forests. "Bone pits" found near several of the forts contained large deposits of crumbling human bones; one pit contained upward of four hundred skeletons.[2] The forts were no doubt created to protect the ancient occupants of the area from a formidable enemy, such as the Lamanites.

In order to explain the Nephite's land northward, it is important to understand that northwestern New York is made up of three steps, or tiers. The first and lowest tier borders the southern shores of Lake Ontario, which terminates abruptly against the steep 250-foot-high Niagara escarpment. The flat Tonawanda plains above the scarp thus make up a second tier in the landscape that terminates against the rather inconspicuous Onondaga escarpment, with the lands above the scarp (Bountiful), creating still a third level. The continuous forestation along the sloping cliffs of the Onondaga escarpment appears to have provided a natural line of demarcation between Bountiful and the land Desolation, just

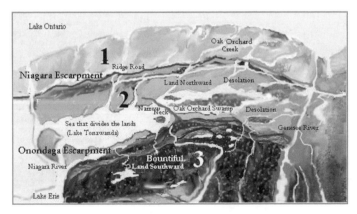

Northwestern New York is made up of 3 tiers.

The Niagara escarpment, which separates the plains along Lake Ontario from the 2nd step up in the landscape.

like the strip of wilderness that separated the land of Nephi from the land of Zarahemla further south. Because the primitive forests along the Onondaga escarpment have never been cut down, they are protected today and are known as Nature's Corridor. Not only does it include one of the largest contiguous wooded corridors in the territory, but it also has a spectacular diversity of plant and wildlife well worth protecting

Limestone ledges along the face of the Onondaga escarpment provide several answers to strange comments made in the scriptures. For instance, in Helaman 14:21–22, Samuel the Lamanite prophesied that all the rocks the Nephites knew to be in one solid mass would all be broken up at the time of the Savior's death. His statement can easily be explained with a quick look at the broken up rock face of the limestone ridges along the escarpment. The Clarendon/Linden Fault actually shows slippage along the scarp during some major earthquake.

The Onondaga escarpment bordering Bountiful is not as high as the Niagara escarpment, although it rises 250 feet near Batavia.

Limestone ledge along the Onondaga escarpment
Courtesy Vincent Coon

Cement, Flint, and Rock Cavities

During Book of Mormon times, those in the land northward used cement to build their cities for a time because the Jaredites had stripped the land of its trees. But where did the inhabitants get this cement? This question can also be answered by the landscape. It seems that the scarp contains an abundance of limestone, a common sedimentary rock often used in the making of cement. Because of the abundance of limestone and gypsum in the scarp, settlers who moved into the area in 1829 started a thriving cement industry that prospered for decades.

The scarp also contains significant outcrops of flint, a kind of chert that was highly sought after for arrowheads and spear points during ancient times. A flint quarry was recently discovered just to the north of Batavia where the Tonawanda Creek pours over the scarp at Indian Falls. The great majority of arrowheads and spear points, wherever they were found in New York, were made from this high-grade western New York Onondaga flint.

Another interesting correlation between text of the Book of Mormon and the terrain of western New York is the fact that the scarp has several limestone caves that were carved out by the constant flow of water over the scarp and onto the plains below. It is easy to imagine that the prophet Ether used such a cave during the Jaredites's final days of warfare. The scriptures

The prophet Ether

tell us he ventured out only at night to view the destruction of his people, something easily done from the elevated position of the scarp where he could see the burning villages below. In fact, by walking the crest of the scarp, he could view the destruction of his people all the way to the Genesee River, just a little to the west of the hill Ramah/Cumorah.

—⚬ 10 ⚬—

The Land Northward

Moving north from Bountiful at an elevation of 900 feet, would have taken the Nephites north over the Onondaga escarpment and onto the flat plains below at an elevation of 650 feet. Those who chose to move even farther north would have moved down over the Niagara escarpment and onto the lower plains bordering Lake Ontario, which lies at an elevation of 350 feet, although the lower plains were pretty marshy back then and filled with low-lying waters called fenlands. The land northward appears to have incorporated the fertile lowlands along the entire northern tier of New York and beyond into Canada for Alma 50:11 claims, the Nephites possessed all the land north of Bountiful "according to their pleasure."

On the flat plains below Bountiful was an ancient lake called Lake Tonawanda. While we have no picture of old Tonawanda, the beach strands it

Modified USGS map

The Western New York setting for the Book of Mormon

left behind indicates it stretched across the plains for fifty-eight miles, was six miles wide at its widest, and discharged over the Niagara escarpment in five separate falls near Lewiston, Lockport, Gasport, Median, and Holly. In time, four of the lake's five spillways closed, leaving only the one at Lewiston near the present site of Niagara Falls to carry the discharge from Lake Tonawanda over the Niagara escarpment and out to Lake Ontario.

New York's Department of Geological Sciences, and the Museum of Paleontology at the University of Michigan took radiocarbon samples in 1978 in an area around Niagara Falls. The results led Calkin and Brett to conclude that Lake Tonawanda existed up to one thousand years ago,[1] a full six hundred years after the close of the Nephite era. The Jaredites probably referred to this seas as "the sea that divides the land" (Ether 10:20).

The scriptures also mention a narrow neck

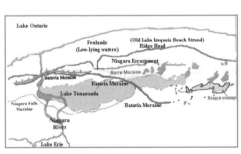

Modified from map by Heidi H. Natel

of land that led from the land southward into the lands to the north. Just such a narrow neck of land was discovered on an old survey map, which revealed a narrow ridge of glacial debris called the Batavia Moraine that extended from Batavia (in northeastern Bountiful), down

Niagara Falls

the Onondaga escarpment and across Lake Tonawanda. This strip of land would have allowed the Nephites easy access to the north shores of the lake where so many opted to settle in hopes of distancing themselves even further from the Lamanites. Although the moraine blends into the surrounding landscape today, it was apparently high enough during Nephite times to act as dam across the shallow end of the lake, allowing dry passage from one side to the other. One has to wonder what better name they could have given it than a narrow neck, a small neck, a narrow pass,

This modified Google Earth view of the area gives an idea of what the narrow neck may have looked like when the water flanked the pass on both sides.

or passageway. It would have been easy for Teancum to head Morianton's men off at the narrow pass as noted in Alma 50:34, because the seas barred the way to either side. Had it been miles and miles wide, it would have taken an army of thousands to successfully block their path.

A number of

75

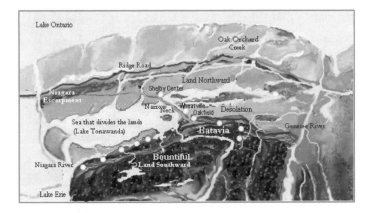

ancient fortifications have been found on both sides of the narrow pass, likely having been built at the insistence of Captain Moroni, who sent orders to Teancum "that he should fortify the land Bountiful, and secure the narrow pass which led into the land northward, lest the Lamanites should obtain that point and should have power to harass them on every side" (Alma 52:9). Teancum obeyed that command.

E. G. Squire noted that ancient forts formed a chain of no less than twenty fortifications from the "Lake Ridge" southward to Buffalo Creek, "a distance of fifty miles."[2]

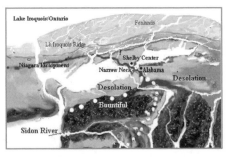

An immense number of bones were found near an ancient fort a little to the west of the modern city of Shelby Center, which lay just to the north of the narrow neck. The skulls were crushed as if by a tomahawk, leading to the common belief that this was once the scene of some great battle. Three other forts were found at the modern city of Alabama, just to the south of the narrow neck, no doubt built to protect the entrance into the land northward. Another fort was discovered at Oakfield between the narrow

Narrow neck of land

neck and Batavia. A large enclosure nearby was named Bone Fort because a mound found within it was made up almost entirely of human bones.

The narrow neck was apparently a thoroughfare for travelers, not just during the Jaredite and Nephite eras, but for those during colonial days as well. In their efforts to connect the lands in the north with those to the south and Buffalo Harbor, the Holland Land Company cut a road that led from Shelby Center, southward to Batavia and Buffalo Road, and from there westward to the harbor at Buffalo.

While the city of Bountiful in Nephite times was one of the most prominent cities in the land southward, the city of Desolation was one of the most prominent cities in the land northward. It was built near the narrow neck, a perfect position to facilitate trade with merchants and hunters who moved back and forth between

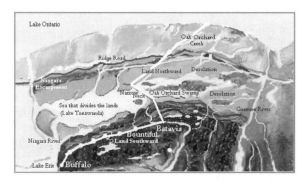

Roads that connected the land northward and southward during colonial days likely connected the two territories during Nephite times as well.

the lands northward and southward. The city of Teancum was also likely built along the shores of Lake Tonawanda, because the scriptures place it near the "seashore" (Mormon 4:3). Other nearby cities included Boaz and Jordan, proving that many of those who moved northward had no intentions of settling any further north than around the shores of old Lake Tonawanda, where they still had close communication with their families and friends back in Zarahemla.

Shipping also helped keep communications open, with people moving back and forth across the various waters in the territory to visit and trade with one another. The scriptures say that Hagoth constructed his ship on the borders of Bountiful, by Desolation, and near the narrow neck where the lush forests of Bountiful could provide the timber he needed. No timber could be found farther northward, because the Jaredites had stripped the land northward of its forests. This would place him just to the south of Lake Tonawanda near the Batavia Moraine, or the narrow neck of land.

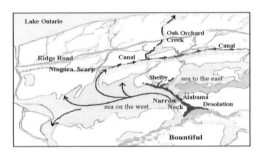

Hagoth built his ship on the borders of Bountiful, by Desolation, near the narrow neck and launched it forth into the west sea, which led into the land northward.

> And it came to pass that Hagoth . . . went forth and built him an exceedingly large ship, on the borders of the land Bountiful, by the land Desolation, and launched it forth into the west sea, by the narrow neck which led into the land northward.
>
> And behold, there were many of the Nephites who did

enter therein and did sail forth with much provisions, and also many women and children; and they took their course northward. And thus ended the thirty and seventh year. (Alma 63:5–6)

Once his ship was completed, Hagoth's crew likely maneuvered it along the lower course of Tonawanda Creek, right into Lake Tonawanda's western basin, where the scriptures say they set their course northward. The area from the narrow neck to Niagara Falls is thirty-two miles, more than twice the length of the thirteen-mile-long Sea of Galilee. Thus this was not just a short jaunt across a small lake, but a major movement of people across a lake of considerable length, with settlements and villages no doubt dotting its north shores where people could sail out into the lake and fish.

Ships heading north may have simply been headed for some of the villages built along the lake's north shore. Yet others may have maneuvered their ship into the deep drainage channel that carried the outflowing waters of both Lake Tonawanda and Lake Erie east to the Mohawk River, the same channel used in modern times in the construction of the Erie Canal. Although portage may have been needed in places, such a waterway could have carried

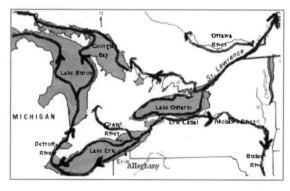

Various waterways would have taken the Nephites to any number of regions.

passengers east all the way to the Mohawk and Hudson Rivers and then south into New England. Others could have diverted their boats into tributary streams and rivers that would have carried them directly into Lake Ontario and from there up the Saint Lawrence River to the maritime regions, north along the Ottawa River into northern Ontario, or west along the Trent River System to Lake Huron. Those sailing south into Lake Erie (the west sea, south) could have moved up the Detroit River to Lake Huron. Thus, any number of routes would have connected the vast numbers of people who opted to move into neighboring regions.

Part Four

The Land of Desolation

During the age of the Jaredites

11

Desolation

The New York landscape was likely one unbroken wilderness when the Jaredites first arrived, with rivers, lakes, and extensive wetlands found all across the land. Artifacts consistent with the Jaredites and their timeline indicate that while they covered a wide expanse of territory, their heartland remained along the Niagara frontier, and between what today are the Niagara and the Genesee Rivers. It is no wonder their history is included in the Book of Mormon, for the Jaredites occupied the same territory as the Nephites, although chiefly in the land northward, having also been brought to the land by the hand of the Lord.

Mastodon

The archaeological record shows arrowheads dating back to the Jaredite era all around Lake Tonawanda. It is believed the extensive swamps on the lake shores existed as far back as Jaredite times, being constantly fed by waters pouring down from the highlands. Oak Orchard Swamp, which is considered to be the last remaining remnant of old Lake Tonawanda, spreads out across the plains for seventeen and a half miles. In the spring, upwards of 100,000 Canadian geese and thousands of ducks rest and feed in the swamps, and small animals roam the wooded areas. Two hundred sixty-six species of birds have been noted in the refuge, and thirty-three species of animals. Deer found in the wooded areas made the swamps a favorite hunting ground.

The Elephant and the Horse

H. L. Fairchild identified some of the extinct animals that once lived the area. He said: "The extinct Pleistocene mammals thus far found in New York are the Mastodon, two or three species of elephant, the peccary, the giant beaver, as large as a black bear; the reindeer and the extinct American horse."[1] Could the mammoth and mastodon be the cureloms and cumoms mentioned in the Jaredite account?

> And they also had horses, and asses, and there were elephants and cureloms and cumoms; all of which were useful unto man, and more especially the elephants and cureloms and cumoms. (Ether 9:19)

Courtesy of New York State Museum

A number of elephant and mammoth skeletons have been discovered in the area's peat bogs and along the Genesee River, which is believed to have been their feeding ground. Interestingly, even homes in modern times have been lost in the mire left behind once the lake began to dry up. Those building on the old lake bed today often find their homes sinking into the layers of oozy clay and sand that creates a kind of quicksand trap. The situation has apparently gotten so bad that legislation is in the works to protect homeowners from contractors who build on the lake bed and neglect to tell buyers of the potential problems they face.

The same soggy conditions may well have existed well into Nephite times. In 4 Nephi 1:9, we learn that entire villages sunk at the time of the Savior's death and that "waters came up in the stead thereof." It could be possible that they sank in the sandy areas where they built on the receding lake shores, only to have the lake replenished by torrents of rain when the terrible tempest hit. Such horrific rainfall would certainly have added to the soggy conditions of the soil, which may have been one of the reasons the Nephites considered the land cursed in the first place.

> Now Lachoneus did cause that they should gather them-
> selves together in the land southward, because of the great
> curse which was upon the land northward. (3 Nephi 3:24)

The soggy condition of the soil in various places in New York as a result of the glacial age may even have been the reason the Nephites lost the treasures they hid up in the earth, never to be found again. Listen to how Mormon describes those events:

> And these Gadianton robbers, who were among the Lama-
> nites, did infest the land, insomuch that the inhabitants
> thereof began to hide up their treasures in the earth; and
> they became slippery, because the Lord had cursed the
> land, that they could not hold them, nor retain them again.
> (Mormon 1:18)

It sounds very much like they slipped right down into the soggy soil. It is no wonder their treasures have remained hidden so long.

The Weather

Regardless of the drawbacks to living in the land northward, the bounties in the land far outweighed the negatives. Even the weather was favorably affected by the swamps. New York State University archaeologist W. A. Ritchie maintains that while the period between 1000 BC and 600 BC was somewhat cooler than the early Jaredite era, which was five degrees warmer, the trend toward the cool, moist climate we know today did not begin to prevail until around the time of Christ.[2] However, the wind is a constant and always seems to blow. Yet the thick tops of the tall trees broke the force of the winds around the swamps, and the softening effects of the Great Lakes in the area prevented the extremes of heat and cold found so prevalent

Snow

in the area today now that so many of the forests have been cut down and many of the wetlands have dried up.[3]

Although the weather was cooler from the time of Christ onward, from the reports given by early settlers during colonial days, it appears the winters were once much milder than they are today. Historians of the seventeenth century claim the old settlers told them the ground seldom froze to the point where a stake could not be easily driven into the earth at any given time. Moreover, it appears from their reports that snow did not fall as much as it sometimes does today.[4]

Nephi actually mentions snow when he was recording the

tree of life: "And the whiteness thereof did exceed the whiteness of the driven snow" (1 Nephi 11:8). Thus, we can conclude that Nephi was familiar with that type of weather. A gentle snow falls in Israel about every seven or eight years, but it melts away rather quickly. Nephi likely did not experience driven snow, the kind that blows in with a snowstorm, until after he arrived in the promised land and secured the ore he needed to record the experiences of his family.

Poisonous Serpents & Fevers

Unfortunately, the stagnant swamps in the area were the perfect breeding ground for a number of health-related problems. Settlers were hit from time to time with a strange ague, which is believed was represented by three separate diseases: malaria, typhus, and typhoid fever—any one of which could be fatal.

The swamps and rivers in the area were also the breeding ground for a number of snakes. The rattlesnake was particularly problematic for early settlers according to old reports, especially along the Niagara, Genesee, and Oak Orchard Rivers. This is another valuable correlation between the scriptures and the western New York setting, for the scriptures say the Jaredites were troubled with poisonous serpents during their era. When the serpents began to bite the domesticated animals of the Jaredites, the animals fled southward, because Lake Tonawanda lay to the north, to the east was the Genesee River, which was also infested with snakes, and the mighty Niagara River barred their way west.

Rattlesnake

Niagara River
courtesy Vincent Coon

Most people do not realize that the Niagara River is as swift at its head as it is where it plunges over the falls at Niagara, for it carries the outflowing waters of all the upper Great Lakes. It was that great volume of water that kept Lake Tonawanda's western basin filled, and the reason the Nephites considered it all part of the same west sea. (In Alma 53:8, the waters in Lake Erie were simply referred to as the "west sea, south.") Most animals are smart enough not to attempt such a perilous crossing, and those that do are often swept over the falls. The only safe place for the animals to go was southward into Zarahemla.

> And there came forth poisonous serpents also upon the face of the land, and did poison many people. And it came to pass that their flocks began to flee before the poisonous serpents, towards the land southward, which was called by the Nephites Zarahemla. (Ether 9:31)

The Sinking Ponds Wildlife Sanctuary appears to have been a particularly popular location of the Jaredites. Six seasonal hunting and fishing grounds were found in the area that have been linked to the Meadowood phase of the Jaredites—a site protected in our day just as it was during Jaredite times, for the Jaredites kept the land southward as a hunting reserve.

To preserve a branch of

Sinking Ponds Wildlife Sanctuary
courtesy Vincent Coon

the initial Jaredite civilization before they all but destroyed themselves in a major civil war, the Lord led King Omer to a place of safety just to the east of the Hill Ramah, right where we find the Montezuma Marsh today. It too is a remnant of the

Montezuma Marsh

last ice age, and was a sea at one time (see Ether 9:3).

Although Omer and his family lived long enough to build up the kingdom again, which thrived for another six hundred years, the final phase of the Jaredites ends as badly as the earlier phase— they too had become ripe in iniquity. Another civil war was on the horizon. Unfortunately, this one was destined to destroy everyone, all but the prophet Ether and Coriantumr, who was told he would live to see another people occupy the land.

As the war commenced, their battles led them eastward to the Hill Ramah, the same hill the Nephites called Cumorah. The scriptures follow them from the city of Moron "down" to the plains below and then a seashore (likely old Tonawanda). Then they went back "up" to the wilderness of Akish, then "down" from

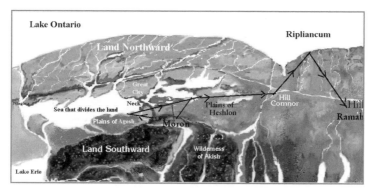

General route taken as Jaredites moved eastward toward the Hill Ramah/Cumorah

the highlands above the scarp to the plains below, and on and on, until we find them heading northeastward toward the waters of Ripliancum, which is interpreted to mean large or exceeding all (Lake Ontario), then ultimately southward to the Hill Ramah where their life's blood was shed.

─◦ 12 ◦─

The Jaredites As Metallurgists

By following the geographical descriptions given in the scriptures, we can place the land of Moron, or the land of the Jaredite's first inheritance, in western New York. However, migrations into neighboring regions began early according to the scriptures, which maintains that various disgruntled Jaredites moved away from time to time, often drawing away a considerable number of people with them.

> And when Corihor was thirty and two years old he rebelled against his father, and went over and dwelt in the land of Nehor; and he begat sons and daughters, and they became exceedingly fair; wherefore Corihor drew away many people after him. (Ether 7:4)

Another land away was the land of Heth, where Omer's wicked son, Jared, enticed half the kingdom to join him (see Ether 8:2). If the land of Heth proves to be Michigan (where many of the Jaredites of the Glacial Kame phase lived), we might wonder if this later, more wicked Jared lured his countrymen into that region by enticing them with promises of great wealth if they worked the copper mines of Michigan's Keweenaw Peninsula. It is often promises of great riches that entice people to leave the comfort of their homes and move to a whole new region. Such a scenario would be similar to the gold rush days of the 1800s when people risked everything to head for the gold mines of California and strike it rich.

> And they did work in all manner of ore, and they did make gold, and silver, and iron, and brass, and all manner of metals; and they did dig it out of the earth; wherefore they did cast up mighty heaps of earth to get ore, of gold, and of silver, and of iron, and of copper. And they did work all manner of fine work. (Ether 10:23)

This scripture makes it clear that the Jaredites were definitely involved in the precious metals being processed in the region, such as copper, gold, silver, and lead. Professor Roy Drier of the Michigan Institute of Mining and Technology believes the five thousand copper mines around Lake Superior dated between 2400 BC and 1200 BC, with a conservative estimate of around twenty to fifty million pounds of copper mined during the Bronze Age. In their book, *The Copper Mines of Lake Superior*, Drier and Du Temple suggest an even larger amount, claiming between 500 million and 1.5 billion pounds of copper were mined in the area during the Bronze Age.[1]

While all the ores mentioned in the Book of Mormon have been noted in Michigan and the regions around the Great Lakes, few realize that the Piedmont gold belt, which resembles the mother lode gold belt in California, stretched along the east coast of America. In fact, the state of North Carolina opened the first commercial gold mining operation in the country, having a particularly large deposit. Large deposits of magnetite-copper ores in Pennsylvania also produced by-product gold, with many massive deposits interspersed between the lode gold deposits. Other ores found in Pennsylvania include lead, zinc, platinum, vermiculite, antimony, zirconium, iron, titanium, uranium, copper, aluminum nickel, lead, and silver, with one lost silver mine thought to be huge. Massive sulfide deposits with copper, or copper and zinc, with by-product gold can also be found in the central Adirondacks of New York, western Massachusetts, eastern Vermont, northern New Hampshire, and Maine. Small deposits of gold were also mined in Ohio, Indiana, Illinois, Wisconsin, Iowa, and Minnesota, with larger deposits in Ontario. Gold production in the eastern and central states into the 1980s yielded upward of fifty million dollars. Who knows how much may have been present during the Nephite and Jaredite eras.

Iron ore is also prevalent western New York, some of it having the quality needed to make steel. Shule went to the hill Ephraim to extract the ore he needed to make steel swords for his men in hopes of restoring his father, King Orihah, to the throne (see Ether 7:9). The hill Cumorah sits in a field of ten thousand small drumlin hills, one of which must have been the hill Ephraim, because the iron ore found in the region is the very type used to make steel.[2] Because of its location so close to the battles around Cumorah, it is highly probable that it was used during the Nephite era to prepare their people with the various weapons of war they needed for their final battles. In more modern times, iron ore has been one of New York's most lucrative export items. Other metals extracted in New York include zinc, lead, silver, and copper, with gold found just to the north of New York in Ontario, Canada.

Metal artifacts were found all across New York during the early years of European colonization. Relics made of iron disintegrated upon being excavated, leaving nothing but traces of rust behind. But some relics found in the mounds, which date to the Nephite era, survived a little better. One mound investigated by a

Mr. Atwater, for instance, contained not only instruments made of stone, but "very well manufactured swords and knives of iron, and possibly steel." Their antiquity was so apparent that he could only conclude that "the primitive people of America, either discovered the use of iron themselves, as the Greeks did, or they carried a knowledge of this ore with them at the time of their dispersion; as received by Noah's family, who brought it from beyond the flood."[3]

Even an understanding of how to make brass was known by the ancients. In Josiah Priest's *American Antiquities* (1838), we learn that a Mr. Halsted plowed up seven or eight hundred pounds of brass "both of husbandry and war" on his farm on Salmon Creek in Scipio.[4] The discovery of such items was commonplace in those days, yet all too often dismissed as being European in origin and therefore discarded. Although brass was no doubt used by the Jaredites for a number of reasons, it appears to have been especially popular in the construction of weapons of war and protective breastplates and headplates. Warfare was a big part of life during the Jaredite era, with much pomp and ceremony going into the burial of their dead.

Unfortunately, most of the burial sites of the Meadowood phase of the Jaredites produced nothing more than ashes, although fragments of bones from four adults show the Meadowood people to be a long-headed race with narrow noses.[5] However, Ritchie believes they were a larger-than-average people, for he found enormous carved antler combs, which ranged in length up to fourteen inches, along with large engraved bone daggers, massive harpoons, and extremely long stone blades amid their grave offerings. Such relics suggested to him that these were "an energetic people imbued with definite and objective ideas."[6] Such a description certainly sounds like the Jaredites, who the scriptures describe as "large and mighty men" (Ether 15:26).

A perfect example of such a large, powerfully built man was noted when a grave was excavated in Hardin County, Ohio, by John S. Matson in 1856. It revealed the skeleton of a man assigned to the Glacial Kame culture, which was described by Matson as the largest he had ever seen. He explained, "The joints of the vertebra seemed as large as those of a horse. I think they did not indicate a taller frame than some others; but the bones were heavier than any in the mound."[7] The discovery of such large bones was so commonplace that the reports of such finds often simply stated, "It is evident that the aborigines of American Indians were much larger than those of other tribes."

Whether some of the Jaredites reached the enormous size of some of the Celtic tribes that migrated to America during the Bronze Age

Jaredite

cannot be determined. A whole cemetery of such large men was discovered in 1871. Three men were digging on a farm on the banks of the Grand River about forty miles west of the Niagara River. The skeletons found were piled in layers, one atop another, some two hundred in number. That incredible discovery was subsequently written up in Toronto's, *The Daily Telegraph,* Wednesday, August 23, 1871, under the heading, "A remarkable sight— Two hundred skeletons of Anakims in Cayuga Township . . . a vast Golgotha opened to view."

A portion of that article read:

These skeletons are those of men of gigantic stature, some of them measuring nine feet, very few of them being less than seven feet. Some of the thigh bones were found to be at least a foot longer than at present known, and one of the skulls being examined completely covered the head an ordinary person. These skeletons are supposed to belong to a race of people anterior to the Indians.[8]

Dozens of burial pits similar to the one mentioned were found nearby, although smaller, with the skulls of the skeletons found within of an enormous size, most showing evidence of a violent death. The trees growing over the various digs showed centuries of growth, proving the giants in the area were far anterior to the local Indian tribes.[9] So many of the skeletons unearthed in the region show evidence of death by violent means that it can hardly be doubted that warfare was very much a part of the Jaredites' lifestyle as rival factions continued to vie for the power and glory of the throne. Consequently, the kingdom passed dissent and intrigue and murder from generation to generation.

Unfortunately, the whole civilization ultimately became so steeped in sin that the Lord began a cleansing. Not only had foreigners brought pagan gods into the land, such as the sun-god Baal, and the Minoan's mother goddess, Ashtoreth, but the Jaredites themselves became obsessed with the secret works of the devil.

> And the people had spread again over all the face of the land, and there began again to be an exceedingly great wickedness upon the face of the land, and Heth began to embrace the secret plans again of old, to destroy his father (Ether 9:26).

Thus, the anger of the Lord was kindled against the Jaredites.

> And they hearkened not unto the voice of the Lord, because of their wicked combinations; wherefore, there began to be wars and contentions in all the land, and also many famines and pestilences, insomuch that there was a great destruction, such an one as never had been known upon the face of the earth. (Ether 11:7)

No matter how many disasters the Lord sent upon the unrepentant, they continued to slip back into their wicked ways. In fact, the robbers were no more wicked than some of the Jaredites. The Lord had the prophet Ether warn them that if they did not repent, he would not just send disease and famines upon them this time, but he would totally wipe them off the face of the earth. He'd simply had enough!

The Prophet Ether tried to explain to the people that this was a land choice above all others, and the place where the Lord would rule the nations from the New Jerusalem for a thousand years of peace, but they simply were not interested. The wickedness of the people was so great by this time that they completely ignored Ether's warnings. Thus, he began to record the history of his people, knowing that it would also be their epitaph. It was not an easy task, for warfare was raging all across the land, and Ether was forced to hide in the cavity of a rock to do his recording as he viewed the awful scenes of destruction around him.

Such a scenario makes it clear that their final days of warfare did not take in a particularly large area, but one small enough that the prophet Ether could view the destruction of his people by night and retire to a cave by day to record what he observed (see Ether 13:14). We can suppose that the two armies' movements as they battled one another did not take in any extended tract of land. But the miles covered were hard, and soldiers on both sides dropped in battle along the way as they moved closer to their final place of extermination on the plains around the hill Ramah/Cumorah. This was no small war—total victory was the goal of both sides.

As was the custom of the time, a period of four years was agreed upon so they could gather together their people from all the outlying regions for one final showdown, for with the winning side went the crown and kingdom. Sadly, neither side prevailed, and the entire nation was destroyed except for two lone men: the prophet Ether, who survived to write the history of his people, and Coriantumr, who lived long enough to see another people (the Mulekites) take possession of the land.

Part Five

People and Migrations

— 13 —

The Merged Nephite and Mulekite Populations

We learn from the scriptures that Mulek escaped Jerusalem when his father, King Zedekiah, was taken captive into Babylon. Gladys Taylor reminds us that while Joseph's role in Israel was important, there were the two leadership roles in Israel: one represented by Judah, who held the scepter, and the other by Joseph, who led in all matters of national importance. Therefore, with Joseph's line destined to arrive in the promised land with the colony of Lehi, it was apparently important for Judah's line to be there too, so that the purposes of the Lord might be fulfilled on both sides of the ocean.

While a number of Israelites fled to Egypt when Israel fell, others found sanctuary in the seaport of Sidon at the east end of the Mediterranean Sea. Others chose the small isle off the mainland, called Tyre, which was almost impregnable. From there, many migrated into various nations throughout Europe and Asia. What route Mulek and his company took is not known, but because the children of Israel were not known for their seafaring

Mulekites

skills, except for the tribe of Dan, it is likely they moved northward from Jerusalem through the wilderness into the seaport at Sidon or Tyre, where they secured passage on a Danite ship that then brought them to the new world.

Davidly Yair maintains that during Solomon's time, Phoenician Tyre was almost exclusively in Israelite power.[1] The Danites were experts in the production of bronze and were no doubt aware of the copper mines of North America. It would not be surprising to learn that a Danite ship transported Mulek and his royal entourage across the sea to America. Perhaps they even had permanent settlements in the area and were aware of the lands left vacant by the Jaredites—lands now free for the taking. While the Jaredites filled much of the lands to the north, the land southward had been kept as a hunting preserve and was still in a pristine state, ready for occupation by these sea-weary travelers.

We learn in the *Journal of Discourses* that the lost 116 pages of the Book of Mormon specified the lineages of those who made it to America, and the possibility that others might have been among them.

> Nephi individually was from the tribe of Manasseh, but that Ishmael was from the tribe of Ephraim, and that his sons married into Lehi's family, and Lehi's sons married

Ishmael's daughters. . . . Thus, the descendants of Manasseh and Ephraim grew together upon this American continent, with a sprinkling from the house of Judah from which Mulek descended, who left Jerusalem eleven years after Lehi and founded the city of Zarahemla found by Mosiah—thus making a combination, an intermixture of Ephraim and Manasseh with the remnants of Judah, and for aught we know, the remnants of some other tribes that might have accompanied Mulek. (Journal of Discourses 23:184–85)

Three routes would have been available to them once they reach America: 1) sailing inland along the Saint Lawrence River directly into Lake Ontario, 2) up the Hudson River and along various inland rivers to Lake Ontario, or 3) up the Mississippi River and through the Great Lakes to Lake Erie, disembarking at the mouth of the Buffalo River, or perhaps further north along the shores of ancient Lake Tonawanda, the fifty-eight-mile-long inland sea the Jaredites referred to as the sea that divided the land. All we know for sure is that the Lord led the Mulekites into the land north—a region originally referred to as the land of Mulek after the son of King Zedekiah, while the Nephites were led into lands further south, which were referred to as the land of Lehi (see Helaman 6:10).

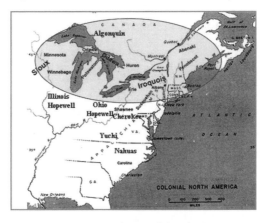

Point Peninsual area of distribution

Point Peninsula heartland

Although the two peoples did not merge until around 130 BC, their cultures were so similar, both having come from Jerusalem at approximately the same time, that New York State archaeologist, William A. Ritchie, simply referred to the culture that emerged in New York around this time as the Point Peninsula culture, named after an island at the east end of Lake Ontario.

After examining various relics and cultural similarities, Ritchie determined that in time the culture covered a wide range, stretching from southern Manitoba and northern Minnesota on the west, as far as Maine, New Hampshire, and New Brunswick on the east, throughout southern New York and New England on the south, and beyond the land which separates the drainage of the Great Lakes from that of Hudson Bay on the north. Yet it is the consensus that the cultural heartland remained in lower Ontario between Lake Huron and Georgian Bay, and in New York from the north shore of Lake Erie (Zarahemla) eastward across central New York's Finger Lakes region to Oneida Lake, with fingers reaching up the Saint Lawrence River to Lake Champlain.[2]

Those who chose to settle in southern Ontario came to be known as the Saugeen people, after the Saugeen River. One Saugeen site near Lake Huron was radiocarbon dated to 668 BC ±220 years. An ancient site along the Saugeen River was dated to 519 BC±60 years. The plus and minus variables make both time lines consistent with the arrival of both the Nephites and

Mulekites—Jerusalem having fallen around 587 BC.

Early researchers initially thought the Saugeen may have been part of an earlier cultural horizon. However, the writers of *The History of the Native People of Canada* are now convinced that the people of the Saugeen regional complex in southern Ontario and the Point Peninsula people of New York shared the same ancestry, but they had simply chosen to live in different geographical locations. Ritchie was also convinced that they were genetically and culturally related and suggests the Saugeen people simply represented a very early phase of the overall culture.

Although the Nephites were relatively safe in Zarahemla once they merged with the Mulekites, conflicts arose from time to time that caused a considerable number of Nephites to move northward. Because the territory to the north of Lake Tonawanda was rather restricted with Lake Ontario stretching out to the north of it, those wishing to expand outward generally moved east into central New York, where some settled around the eleven beautiful Finger Lakes, a region that matches the territory the Book of Mormon describes as "a land of many waters" perfectly. Others moved even farther into a land described as a land of large bodies of water (see Helaman 3:8). While such a description is certainly consistent with the neighboring Great Lakes, it is also consistent with southern Ontario's *Land O' Lakes*, a chain of fourteen lakes

Finger Lakes of central New York

that range in size from two to eighteen square miles. They form a link in a winding system of rivers that connect Georgian Bay to Lake Ontario. The archaeological record shows the Point Peninsula people

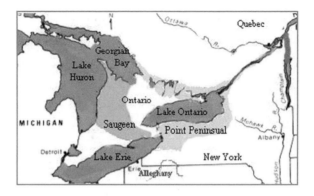

The northward migration of the Nephites into a land of large bodies of water, many rivers, and seas.

ultimately filled every river valley in southern Ontario from Georgian Bay on the north (sea north) to Lake Erie on the south (sea south), and from Lake Huron on the west (sea west) to Lake Ontario on the east (sea east). It appears the seas referred to in Helaman 3:8 were being described in relation to their positions in the land, not by name.

Ritchie believes those who moved northward from their villages in New York chose locations that made trade of such items as copper, silver, and perishable goods easy with those to the south of them. Although the Bronze Age was over, the local use of such precious metals was in high demand during the Nephite era. Silver with copper could be found around Lake Superior, but around two thousand years ago, silver from the Cobalt area in northern Ontario was discovered. In fact, this may have been what caused the population explosion in the area in the first place. The Cobalt silver

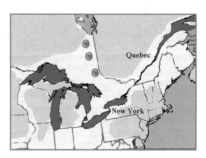

Location of mines represented by circles

mines near Lake Temiskaming produced 460 million ounces of silver in the last century alone. One vein was so large (containing as much as 10,000 tons of processed silver) that it is considered the largest single find in the world, and referred to as the "silver sidewalk." Some veins had pieces of silver as big as stove lids and cannon balls.

A little to the north were gold mines, with gold fever likely bringing more people north. By 2001, the Porcupine Gold Mine produced sixty-seven million ounces of gold, making it by far the largest gold rush in terms of actual gold produced. Even the Klondike Gold Rush in Alaska during the 1800s only produced twelve million ounces. Another gold mine can be found in nearby Timmins on the Mattagami River. But it has the added advantage of having other base metals as well, such as silver, copper, zinc, and nickel. It would be easy to suppose the quest for wealth was at least one reason for the mass migration northward. The scriptures tell us that at one point five thousand men with their wives and children left for the lands northward, which could be well over twenty thousand people (see Alma 63:4).

14

The Iroquois/Algonquin Connection

Over time, the Point Peninsula people (those who survived the battle at Cumorah) developed into the Owasco culture, who then evolved into the later Iroquois tribes. W. A. Ritchie is firm in his conviction that the Iroquois developed in New York from the Late Point Peninsula populations.[1] Some of the earliest tribes the settlers encountered when they arrived on America's northeastern shores were the Iroquois, many of which were noted for their oratory skills and their regard for the Great Spirit, whom they worshiped.

The New England Lenni Lenape were another branch of the family the settlers encountered, although of Algonquin stock. The Algonquins appear to have evolved from the mixed

The Iroquois greeting Champlain along the St. Lawrence River.

Mulekite and Nephite populations who settled in lower Ontario. There are probably a number of reasons the Nephites moved northward, but the main reason, of course, is that the Lamanites barred their movement southward. In the book of Helaman we first heard about those who moved north. Helaman 3:8–16 is the only source that speaks of what became of them. Great changes took place among them in just a few short generations as the Nephites and Lamanites in the land northward began to mix.

Helaman said,

> And it came to pass that they did multiply and spread, and did go forth from the land southward to the land northward, and did spread insomuch that they began to cover the face of the whole earth, from the sea south to the sea north, from the sea west to the sea east. . . .
>
> And it came to pass that there were many of the people of Ammon, who were Lamanites by birth, did also go forth into this land.
>
> And now there are many records kept of the proceedings of this people, by many of this people, which are particular and very large, concerning them.
>
> But behold, a hundredth part of the proceedings of this people, yea, the account of the Lamanites and of the Nephites, and their wars, and contentions, and dissensions, and their preaching, and their prophecies, and their shipping and their building of ships, and their building of temples, and of synagogues and their sanctuaries, and their righteousness, and their wickedness, and their murders, and their robbings, and their plundering, and all manner of abominations and whoredoms, cannot be contained in this work.
>
> But behold, there are many books and many records of every kind, and they have been kept chiefly by the Nephites.
>
> And they have been handed down from one generation to another by the Nephites, even until they have fallen into transgression and have been murdered, plundered, and hunted, and driven forth, and slain, and scattered upon the

face of the earth, and mixed with the Lamanites until they are no more called the Nephites, becoming wicked, and wild, and ferocious, yea, even becoming Lamanites. (Helaman 3:8–16)

It is interesting to remember how the Nephite apostate Jacob fled to the northernmost part of the kingdom with his followers. There he hoped to build a kingdom of his own until they were strong enough to fight and kill the Nephites, a plan that apparently worked centuries later when those who affiliated themselves with the Lamanites came against the Nephites and totally destroyed them.

> Therefore, Jacob seeing that their enemies were more numerous than they, he being the king of the band, therefore he commanded his people that they should take their flight into the northernmost part of the land, and there build up unto themselves a kingdom, until they were joined by dissenters, (for he flattered them that there would be many dissenters) and they become sufficiently strong to contend with the tribes of the people; and they did so. (3 Nephi 7:12)

Perhaps Jacob's band initiated the culture that evolved into the later Laurel culture of northern Ontario. The archaeological record also ties the Laurel people to the Point Peninsula populations. Laurel settlement sites have been traced from the border of Quebec across northern Ontario, throughout much of Manitoba and east-central Saskatchewan, and as far south as Michigan and Minnesota. While much about these people is still unknown, there is consensus that Laurel pottery is related to the pottery of both the Point Peninsula and Saugeen cultures of southern Ontario. The carefully modeled and decorated pottery vessels of the Laurel people share so many traits with the Saugeen and Point Peninsula people that the authors of *The History of the Native People of Canada* report it is frequently difficult to distinguish between the two cultures on the basis of pottery alone.

While Canadian archaeologists maintain that all the Algonquin-speaking people of northern Ontario descended from the Laurel and are known by a variety of names, they are generally recognized under the names Algonkin, Ojibway, and Cree. Today, the Ojibway are the third largest group of Native Americans in the United States, surpassed only by the Cherokee and the Navajo.

William Warren, who spent many years observing the Ojibway and their way of life, said:

> The more I have become acquainted with their [Ojibway] anomalous and difficult to be understood character—the more insight I have gained into their religious and secret rites and faith, the more strongly has it been impressed on my mind that they bear a close affinity or analogy to the chosen people of God, and they are either descendants of the lost tribes of Israel, or they have had, in some former era, a close contact and intercourse with Hebrews, imbibing from them their beliefs and customs and the traditions of their patriarchs.[2]

It is interesting to note that the Ojibway are known for writing on birch bark scrolls. They are said to be the keepers of the tribal records, their poems and dreams, and responsibilities that the scriptures generally give the Nephites rather than the Lamanites, which may give us a hint about their lineage.

Even the language of the Algonquins can be traced back to the Nephites who ultimately moved north. In 1967, Frank Siebert determined that the origins of the Proto-Algonquin language could be traced to the Saugeen and Point Peninsula people living in southern Ontario between Georgian Bay and Lake Ontario as far south as Niagara Falls[3]—the very place the Nephites who moved northward ultimately came to settle. Dr. Cyclone Covey went so far as to claim the Algonquin language prevailed "universally over all North America north of Mexico, from the Atlantic to the

*Champlain's drawing of a war between the Iroquois
and Algonquins, both of which were entirely naked.*

Rockies" and was the language of the Hopewell.[4] Anthropologists
tell us this could not have happened without a written language,
notwithstanding different dialects developed in various regions.

Interestingly, the most often asked question about the northern setting is about the weather, supposing it was too cold for
the Lamanites to have worn nothing but loincloths. However, the
Algonquins dressed in the same way their ancient fathers did centuries before, with nothing but a loincloth, even in harsh weather.
The French explorer Champlain actually described the Iroquois
and Algonquians in his writings and drawings in 1602 as going
entirely naked in a battle waged in mid-Octocber.

As the various northern tribes migrated away from their heartland, they moved along every river in the territory, giving each settlement they founded a different archaeological name. Although
one thousand miles separated those in Illinois and New York, "so
strikingly similar are some of the pottery types shared by these
widely separated cultures" that Don Dragoo "believed a direct
generic relationship seems to have existed."[5] The archaeological
record has since proven him right, indicating a direct relationship between the Havana Culture in Illinois, the Laurel culture of

northern Ontario, the Saugeen of southern Ontario, and the Point Peninsula culture of New York.

In time, the merged blood of Lehi and Mulek was spread throughout the entire northeast from Canada to the Gulf Coast. The DNA X haplogroup, which has recently been tied to the Near East and also Israel, shows definite ties to several tribes throughout the country. The Algonquin carrying it at the highest levels at 25 percent, and the Ojibway at 20 percent. The Iroquois carry it at frequencies of 15 percent, the Nuu-Chah-Nulth along the northwest coast of Canada at frequencies of 11–13 percent, the Navajo in Arizona, Utah, and New Mexico at 7 percent, and the Yakima in Washington at 5 percent,[6] showing just how far the Nephites and Lamanites traveled, merging bloodlines all along the way.

Dean R. Snow maintains that the Algonquian-speaking people also carried the Point Peninsula culture into New England,[7] where we find other tribes such as the Lenni Lenape, considered the grandfathers of them all.

Today the Iroquois speak a different language than the Algonquins. However, we might remember that when the Nephites joined the Mulekites in Zarahemla they could not understand them because they had neglected to bring their records with them

*William Penn signing a treaty
with the Lenni Lenape*

and had lost their mother tongue. The Nephites taught them their language once they merged; however, some in outlying regions may never have had the opportunity. Yet, regardless of language differences, Ritchie claims the Owasco culture that evolved from the New York–based Point Peninsula populations (which we can take to be the victorious Lamanites who destroyed their Nephite bothers in AD 384) were once made of various groups included both the Algonquins and the Iroquois.[7]

$\sim\!\!\diamond$ **15** $\diamond\!\!\sim$

Nephite-Type Writing

The Point Peninsula populations have also been traced from their center in New York and lower Ontario east of the Saint Lawrence River to Champlain Lake and across northern New Hampshire and Maine into New Brunswick. Among the eastern tribes we find evidence of the Nephite's writing system. Scholars have traced the Algonquin language from the east coast of North America to the Rocky Mountains. The Proto-Algonquin language, from which all those in the area descended, was spoken for the past 2,500 years with no one yet able to tie it linguistically to other languages of the world, a curious fact made more understandable when one learns that the Nephites altered their pattern of speech and writing.

> And now, behold, we have written this record according to our knowledge, in the characters which are called among us the reformed Egyptian, being handed down and altered by us, according to our manner of speech.
>
> And if our plates had been sufficiently large we should have written in Hebrew; but the Hebrew hath been altered

by us also; and if we could have written in Hebrew, behold, ye would have had no imperfection in our record.

But the Lord knoweth the things which we have written, and also that none other people knoweth our language; and because that none other people knoweth our language, therefore he hath prepared means for the interpretation thereof. (Mormon 9:32–34)

While the Lord prepared interpreters to help translate the record of the Nephite people into the Book of Mormon, evidence is surfacing that ties the language of the Algonquins of the northeast to the language of Egypt, the very place the tribes of Israel were held in bondage to Pharaoh for four hundred years.

Evidence that the Mi'kmaq (Micmac) branch of the Algonquin family in New Brunswick and Maine preserved the Nephites' ancient hieroglyphic style of writing was first recognized in 1610 when Catholic monks taught the aboriginal tribes in the region about Christianity. But while teaching them, they discovered that the Micmac wrote in a form of Egyptian hieroglyphics, which has led to a considerable amount of controversy.

After extensive study of the Micmac hieroglyphics, the epigrapher Barry Fell could see a definite connection between the Algonquians and Egypt. But not knowing about the Nephites and that they wrote in reformed Egyptian, he could only wonder if maybe Egyptians may have occupied the region at some remote time in history. He was so amazed by the remarkable connection between the hieroglyphic writing of the Algonquins and Egyptians that he was surprised "no one until now seems to have noticed it."

He first encountered the similarities while studying a document found in a book written by Eugene Vetromile, containing *The Lord's Prayer* written in Micmac hieroglyphs. Being an authority on ancient languages, Fell was mystified to note that the meaning of the "signs in Egyptian matched the meaning assigned them in the English transcript of the Micmac text given on the document." He learned that some of the early Christian missionaries probably invented such signs in an effort to teach the Indians more effectively. But the evidence before him convinced him that someone with a definite understanding of Egyptian had taught the Micmac how to write.

The scriptures are clear on the manner of writing used by the Nephites and their ties to the language of Egypt.

> Yea, I make a record in the language of my father, which consists of the learning of the Jews and the language of the Egyptians. (1 Nephi 1:2)

Scholars have consistently insisted that the Micmac language is not related to ancient Egyptian but is a purely Native America language related to the Ojibway, Lenape, and Cree. But after studying literally hundreds of Egyptian hieroglyphics, Fell was

Nephite	Mi'kmaq		Nephite	Mi'kmaq
ϟ	ᶜᑊ		𝟚	3
ϲ	ϲ		𝓏	᷑
ϳ	ϳ		8	℘
ᶘ	ᶚ		℘	℘
⸶	⊕		ʌ	△
ᵔ	ᷱ		ℋ	ℋ
ᶚ	℔		Ɗ	℟
ϸ	⸴		𝓏	𝓏
ᴖ	ᴗ		ϛ	Ɛ

The above Nephite symbols, acquired by Vincent Coon, came from the "caractors" transcript, which is an early Mormon transcript of characters copied from the Book of Mormon plates.

Caractors transcript

totally convinced "the Micmac writing system, (and also part of their language), was derived from ancient Egyptian." Yet "how could this be?" he wondered. Surely Maillard had not deciphered the Egyptian language himself, for he had never even been to Egypt, nor had ever been involved in any such activity. Moreover, Maillard died in 1762, sixty-one years before Champollion published his first translation of the Egyptian hieroglyphics. Further, it was quite apparent that the Micmac writing system was not a modern invention but had been among the natives for "who knows how long."

When the first Christian missionaries began their instructions to the Micmacs, they noticed the children were making signs on birchbark, which they explained was an attempt to record what the priests were saying. The Wabenaki Indians in Maine were apparently doing the same thing. The Indians claim that "by these signs they could express any idea with every modification, just as we do with our writings." They informed them further that all the various Indian tribes used this same method of writing to communicate with others, both sending and receiving answers in the same way.

The mystery of how the Micmacs and others came to read and write in Egyptian hieroglyphics intrigued the epigrapher Barry Fell, and he began an intensive study of the matter. The librarians at Harvard helped him gather every available book and paper written on the Micmac and Wabanaki Indians. The Indians themselves had libraries of stone tablets and pieces of bark, and their medicine men had large manuscripts of these peculiar hieroglyphs, which they read over the sick. Father Vetromile records that similar writing was employed by all the northern Algonquin tribes, not just the Micmacs. Moreover, it is said that Ojibway chiefs keep circular copper plates buried with their family history recorded in hieroglyphics.

In responding to the frequent question of whether Micmac and related Algonquins were the descendants of ancient settlers from Egypt, Fell said no, explaining that their language was uniquely Algonquin, although there were certain vocabulary similarities with the Egyptian. In regards to the writing system of the Algonquin, he could only conclude, after extensive research, that it was quite ancient, especially for those in the northeast.[1]

In spite of so much evidence in that direction, scholars are convinced that the Micmac language is not related to ancient Egyptian but is a purely Native America language related to the Ojibway, Lenape, and Cree. It was after studying hundreds of Egyptian hieroglyphics that Fell became convinced that "the Micmac writing system, and also part of their language, was derived from ancient Egyptian." While we can agree with earlier assessments that the Micmac language was a purely native language related to the Ojibway, Lenape, and Cree, we must also agree with Fell, who noted its origins definitely had ties to Egypt.

As the people of Nephi expanded into unknown territories, each group kept their own histories, because it would have been impossible for the scribes in Zarahemla to record the happenings of their people scattered over such an extensive area.

Part Six

The Hopewell

∽ **16** ∽

The Mound Builders

The identity of the Mound Builders was a fascinating subject in the eighteenth and nineteenth centuries as colonists began to settle in the Ohio and Mississippi river valleys. Everywhere they turned, the land was covered with strange mounds of earth, and every time they tried to plow their fields, some relic of the past was unearthed. The identity and origins of the ancient race that created these works puzzled laymen and scientists alike, with a number of theories arising.

After his own study of the matter, Cyrus G. Gordon in his twelfth annual report of the antiquities of the area to

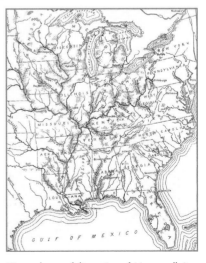

General area of disruption of Hopewell sites throughout the eastern third of the country.

the Smithsonian Institute, concluded that "the ancient tumuli (mounds) of the eastern half of the United States are the remains of a people more highly cultured than the Indian tribes who were found by the white man, and who had vanished from the country anterior to the Columbian discovery." Although his ideas were thought to be romantic and fanciful by those who insisted the mounds were built by the Indians, his work proves to be right, for recent DNA now ties the Ohio Hopewell to the Algonquins, and thus back to the Nephites and Mulekites.

During his own research of the mound cultures, James Griffin noted that 90 percent of the ceramic material in the Ohio Hopewell complexes were northern in origin, with interesting parallels to the pottery of the Point Peninsula populations. However, because so few Hopewell relics show up in New York, Don Dragoo determined it must have been their close relatives living directly above Ohio who participated in the developing mound cultures of Ohio.[1] We are once again led to the populations living in lower Ontario where so many Nephites moved north among the Mulekites and ultimately became Lamanites, or Proto-Algonquin.

Note: Along with foreign DNA, Lisa A. Mills maintains that DNA samples taken from the Ohio Hopewell Mound Group shares some degree of relatedness with Native American tribes such as the Ojibway/Chippewa, Kickapoo, Micmacs, Iowa, and the Pima, and the Apache, Pawnee, Seri, southwest Sioux and Yakima.[2]

The Adena

The earliest mound culture in Ohio is referred to as the Adena culture. DNA evidence ties the Adena back to the Glacial Kame people (the Michigan-based Jaredites) and a people from Illinois referred to as the Red Ocher culture, who together formed the core stock from which the Adena populations emerged.[3] The

Adena culture existed from 1000 to 100 BC in a variety of locations, including Ohio, Indiana, West Virginia, Kentucky, and parts of Pennsylvania and New York. Don Dragoo maintains that the most conspicuous trait donated by Red Ocher to the Central Basin was the practice of erecting small mounds to bury their dead.[4]

As the Nephites and Mulekites arrived in the New World and spread out in all directions, including Ohio, the Adena migrated into a variety of other regions. Archaeologists have traced some to the south of the Ohio River, others to Chesapeake Bay, and still others to the Point Peninsula's eastern Great Lakes trade areas. W. A. Ritchie traced them from Ohio into Delaware, New Jersey, central and eastern New York and New England via the Delaware, Hudson, and Connecticut Rivers where he suggests they "obtain[ed] tenure, either by force or more probably by consent of the local residents, with whom in time they were culturally and physically assimilated"—the host culture being the Point Peninsula populations.[5] A less well-defined route along the Ohio and Allegheny Rivers led from the parent area in Ohio into western and central New York as well. The Middlesex focus in New York and New England are thought to represent "infusion of the Adena culture . . . into regional native cultures of the northeast,"[6] which may go far in explaining why the New England Lenni Lenape are referred to as "Grandfathers," because the Glacial Kame ancestry of the Adena, with whom the Lamanites likely mixed, would have given them the distinction of having a more ancient ancestry than their northern Algonquin brothers. Their tall stature may also be a result of such a merger. European settlers described the Lenape as tall, broad-shouldered, strong people with dark eyes and straight black hair.

The Ohio Hopewell

Although the early mound culture of the Adena back in Ohio was not as grand as their Hopewell predecessors, Griffin believes the Adena culture in central Ohio produced a type culture that was so attractive to the people in the north that there was an actual movement of people southward from New York, from lower Ontario, and from the northwest and Illinois into Ohio, "where they blended with Adena to produce the Ohio Hopewell."[7]

The term *Hopewell* simply refers to a wide system of trade involving the exchange of ideas and goods between various related groups scattered over a broad area of eastern North America. "The increasing body of radiocarbon dates available suggest 100 BC as an approximate beginning for the Interaction Sphere, and AD 300–350 for its attenuation."[8]

Three types of pottery show up in the Hopewell tradition: those with ties to Illinois, a second type from New York's Point Peninsula populations, and a third from the southeast, where the bulk of the Nahuas lived. In fact, H. H. Bancroft believed it was likely the Nahuas who actually initiated the Hopewell mound culture. Edward McMichael boasts of having indisputable evidence of a Floridian migration to Ohio. He maintains that about AD 1, or shortly before, the Mexican State of Veracruz contributed a complex of cultural traits to the northwest coast of Florida, which inspires the Crystal River Complex.[9] The people moved north following the trade routes into Ohio, where they built the same platform-type mounds as those back home. McMichael believes it was this culture from the Crystal River temple complex in Florida that added the fluorescence and elevated the Ohio Hopewell complex into elaborate ceremonial centers.

As to the mounds themselves, Stephen D. Peet said:

> The earth-works of Ohio were designed to protect the villages . . . but they were villages which were pervaded by sun

worship. . . . They went to the fields, to the dance grounds, to the places of assembly, to the ponds and streams and springs under its protection, and even placed their dead in graves or upon altars which were symbolic of the sun. When they conducted war, they brought back their captives, kept them for a time in enclosures consecrated to the sun, and afterwards immolated them as victims and perhaps presented their bodies or hearts as offerings to the sun, making the remarkable terraced mounds the place where this chief rite was celebrated. The platform mounds may have been foundations for temples; they were, however, temples which were depositories for the bodies of their eminent men, rather than assembly places, and were approached by great and solemn procession, the graded and covered ways having been built for the express purpose of accompanying these ceremonies.[10]

Archaeologists noted four major changes in Ohio when the Hopewell culture began to rise around 100–50 BC: "(1) The rise of a strong socio-religious ruling class constituting a selected minority of the population; (2) an elaboration and centralization of the functions of the mortuary cult by the ruling class; (3) the establishment of a more effective social organization that brought the general population under the control of the ruling class, thus making possible the group labor necessary for the construction of large burial mounds and earthworks; and (4) a general population increase."[11]

We glimpse the culture that caused such a stir among the Nephites from the Book of Mormon where Alma mentions that an entirely different religious order entered the land around 91 BC, an order referred to as the order of Nehor. It appears Nehor, the man who introduced the order, was preaching priestcraft among the people. The scriptures describe him a large man and "noted for his much strength" (Alma 1:2). We can suppose he was of Scythian or Celtic stock, many of which reached enormous size and were noted for their strength. Once arriving in Zarahemla, he faced Alma, who was not only aware of Nehor's intentions of introducing the Nephites to a new religious order, but was also alarmed by the idea.

> But Alma said unto him: Behold, this is the first time that priestcraft has been introduced among this people. And behold, thou art not only guilty of priestcraft, but hast endeavored to enforce it by the sword; and were priestcraft to be enforced among this people it would prove their entire destruction. (Alma 1:12)

Actually, the Celts and their Druid priests may have already infiltrated Zarahemla, for those who did not belong to the Church indulged themselves in "sorceries, and in idolatry or idleness, and in babblings, and in envyings and strife; wearing costly apparel; being lifted up in the pride of their own eyes; persecuting, lying, thieving, robbing, committing whoredoms, and murdering, and all manner of wickedness" (Alma 1:32), the same traits found among the Celts, who were known for their robbing and plundering ways, and whose Druid priests paid homage to the sun-god Bel, not the Savior. They discounted the Savior and his atoning sacrifice and believed the only true and perfect atonement of one's sins was the sacrifice of their lives—similar ideas practiced by the people who ascribed to the order of Nehor in Ammonihah.

> But as to the people that were in the land of Ammonihah, they yet remained a hardhearted and a stiffnecked people; and they repented not of their sins, ascribing all the power of Alma and Amulek to the devil; for they were of the profession of Nehor, and did not believe in the repentance of their sins. (Alma 15:15)

It becomes readily apparent why Alma was so upset when Nehor penetrated Nephite territory and taught that men needed no repentance, because in the end, he claimed, all men would have eternal life (see Alma 1:4). Alma could see right from the start that Nehor's philosophies and false teachings would lead to the complete destruction of his people. Thus, when Nehor began to enforce his views with the sword, Alma condemned him to die. Unfortunately, even after his death, others of his kind perpetuated his teachings and drew away many people after them.

Whatever the Nehors patterned their order after, it was an abomination to the Lord, and the followers of Christ continually tried to rid the land of it. The Nephites who embraced the order of Nehor moved south into Lamanite territory where the order was flourishing among the Amalekites and the descendants of the wicked priests of King Noah. From there, we can suppose, they went into Ohio among the rising Hopewell populations.

Between the first century BC and the third century AD, the Hopewell spread from its main cultural and ceremonial center in Ohio and Illinois into small, trading subcenters found through-out the eastern United States, all ruled by a super chief referred to as the "Great Sun," likely from Newark, Ohio. The righteous Nephites in New York could only cling to their worship of Christ and do their best to avoid the Lamanites who wanted to kill them and the Hopewell who wanted to convert them to their sun-wor-shiping ways.

Treasure Beneath
the Mounds

The Hopewell elite took control of the indigenous populations in Ohio and Illinois by introducing the caste system
and ancestral worship. Dragoo believes that they then turned the
river-bottom settlements into workshops to produce the wealth
that went into the mounds of their great chieftains and employed
the less-cultured
populations as cheap
labor to build them.

A tremendous
number of man-
hours would have
been needed to
construct the great
earthen monu-
ments found across
the land. By way of
example, Shetrone

The Grave Creek Mound
Squire & Davis, American Antiquities

Human head effigy
Squire & Davis

calculates that "the Seip Mound, with a cubic content of 20,000 yards, should be built by fifty workmen in 1,000 days." Computing the cubic contents of all the mounds and earthworks in the state of Ohio to be 30 million cubic yards, he said, "A thousand men working 300 days in the year, each contributing the equivalent of one wagonload of earth daily, would accomplish the task of building them within a century . . . and when it is applied to the probable 100,000 artificial earthworks of the entire mound area, the aggregate of labor, energy, and industry becomes surprising to contemplate."[1]

Artifacts with the most artistic designs were interred with the dead as grave offerings, sometimes including hundreds, even thousands, of pearls. The scriptures themselves make mention of pearls, claiming, "there began to be among them those who were lifted up in pride, such as the wearing of costly apparel, and all manner of fine pearls, and of the fine things of the world" (4 Nephi 1:24). We should not be surprised to note that freshwater pearls could be found all along the Mississippi and Ohio Rivers and their tributaries in ancient times, which were a highly prized commodity among the Hopewell. Tales of pearls of

Hopewell pottery
John Baldwin, The Mound Builders, 1892

great size and beauty spread throughout the land during the early years of European exploration, which led to the plunder of thousands of mounds. De Soto noted one explorer who came upon a mound that produced 350 pounds of the gem. Tragically, in the wake of such a discovery, untold numbers of mounds were destroyed in the search for more.

Thousands of pearls were found in a mound that may have housed the dead of a royal family. It was found in the central mound of the Seip Group, the second highest of the known Hopewell mounds. Inside was a sepulchre or vault, constructed of logs. Four adult skeletons were within accompanied by two infants. Whether they were royalty cannot be determined, but they were definitely among

Pottery vessels
Squire & Davis, 1848

the elite, for the burial was accompanied by a vast array of artifacts, including thousands of pearls and numerous implements and ornaments of copper, mica, tortoiseshell, and silver. The adult male was adorned with a copper nose and a rodlike hair ornament. Even the imprints of its royal robe were apparent, under which was a copper breastplate. The royal robe, or shroud, was of woven fabric with colored designs in tan, maroon, and black.[2] The necklace, which was remarkably well preserved by the salts of the copper, the finest ever taken from an archaic burial, consisted of 332 pearls. Enormous amounts of grave offerings were laid alongside the dead before the mound was raised.

Regarding the mounds and various earthworks, archaeologist S. D. Peet notes that they differed with the region. He states that the northernmost districts were occupied by totemistic hunter tribes who settled chiefly in the forest belt around the Great

Lakes. Still in the north, but in different districts, were those Peet classes as military. He claimed the region was especially adapted to warlike races, with the forests giving too much opportunity for assault to avoid it. He followed this military class into the hill country of New York, Pennsylvania, West Virginia, and along the banks of Lake Erie into the state of Michigan, those we would class as Nephites and Lamanites. In the central districts were a class of agriculturists who were pyramid builders, sun-worshipers, and idolaters.[3]

Aside from the grand ceremonial centers used by the Hopewell as places for instruction in both religious and secular matters, the burial mounds were still the preeminent earthwork of the Hopewell. Ten thousand burial mounds were found in Ohio alone. In some cases they were added upon by each generation until they reached heights of forty to sixty feet, with some containing the remains of a thousand members of a single family line, spanning sometimes centuries. In time, the Hopewell spread across the entire upper Mississippi River Valley, generally in search of materials for their elaborate grave offerings. They shipped goods from one place to another on every navigable river in the land, including the entire length of the Mississippi, the Arkansas, the Ohio, and the Missouri. Silverberg claims they traded well beyond the midwestern heartland, from the Great Lakes, southward to the Appalachians, westward to the Rockies, and southwestward to the Gulf Coast, showing what a "wide net the Hopewell were able to cast."[4]

They even sailed seaworthy vessels on regular excursions to the Gulf of Mexico to exchange goods with those in the Yucatan Peninsula. Trade items included elaborate jeweled ornaments such as conch shell earrings, obsidian knives, copper bracelets, and mica pendants fashioned by skilled Hopewell artisans. In return the Hopewell came home with equally impressive jade statues, gold jewelry, and colorful textiles.

In speaking of the Mound Builders and their differences from the later Indian tribes, Stephen D. Peet said:

Preceding these tribes [Native Americans] we find a certain barbaric magnificence that might be compared to that of the early inhabitants of Great Britain—the symbols of sun-worship wrought into copper and placed upon the bodies. We have no doubt that the persons who were buried here, and who carried such massive axes and wore such heavy helmets and elaborate coats of mail, were ancient sun-worshipers, differing entirely from the later Indians.[5]

Peet was continually amazed by the remarkable resemblance of the symbols found in the Hopewell complexes to the symbols found in the Druid's earthworks in the British Isles. In speaking of them he said:

> These, by aid of the ferry across the river, must have been the scene of extensive religious processions, which can be compared to nothing better than the mysterious processions of the Druid priests which once characterized the sacrifices to the sun among the ancient works of Great Britain. [6]

The evidence is overwhelming that the Hopewell were a multinational society, all of which were sun-worshipers, with only the Nephites back in Zarahemla abstaining from that forbidden practice. It was only after they too gave way to the sinful ways of the Hopewell that the Nephites were finally destroyed.

18

The Cherokee
and Sioux Connection

Mounds can be found all along the Mississippi River and her tributaries, especially the large conical burial mound that made up much of the landscape of ancient northeastern America. The nations following the flood built such mounds, including the Carthaginians, the Greeks, the Romans, Phoenicians, Egyptians, and Jews. Any one of them could have brought the mound culture to America, including those who came with Lehi and Mulek. Mounds acted as places of worship in ancient Israel before the great temple of Solomon was finished. But once that sacred edifice was completed, their "high places" were supposed to be torn down and abandoned but were not. The children of Israel could not seem to break away

Grave Creek Mound

from that tradition and, just as the Lord feared, such "high places" ultimately became places of idol and ancestral worship, just like those of the pagan tribes around them. To make matters worse, they were desecrating such places of worship with the bodies of the dead.

At an early period of world history, a small mound of earth served as both a sepulchre and an altar for the officiating priest to stand upon so the surrounding audience could see him. Such works can be traced from Wales to Russia. In the year 1800, Dr. Adam Clarke wrote a book on his travels from St. Petersburg to the Crimea, and his travels in Russia, Tartary, and Turkey. The mounds he found in those regions he claims are the tombs of the ancient world, and those found in North and South America of the same type are constructed by the ancient Indo-European races of eastern Asia.[1]

The Indo-European culture that existed from Germany eastward to the steppes of Russia are referred to as the Kurgan. They are thought by many authorities to be the proto Indo-European culture from which all Indo-European cultures descended. The word *kurgan* itself means barrow, or mound, in Turkic, referring to a mound of earth heaped over a burial chamber complete with grave goods and sacrificial offerings.

Scythian Saka monuments were similar to those of the Kurgan culture, both of which had common features and sometimes common genetic roots. The Scythian-Saka are grouped with the southern fringe of the Magog's Scythian family of large statured, blond, or redheaded descendants, many of which ultimately settled in Iran, Persia, and India. Dr. J. E. Price maintains that the Saka in Indo-Asia in ninth century BC were "linked to the Iranian priesthood, the Magi."[2] However, Vedic records describe them as lower class red-skinned barbarians, which suggests there were two classes among them.

The Celts and Scythians who had trade routes along the Mississippi were no doubt affilitated with the mound cultures of America. Noting their large size and strength, the rebellious children of Laman and Lemuel were likely only too willing to join them, thinking they would be powerful allies to have. The Sioux tribes, a detached branch of the Iroquois whose DNA ties them to the Hopewell mound builders, are some of the tallest people in the country. The white Lamanite Zelph, whose bones were found in a mound in Illinois by the men of Zion's Camp, measured eight or nine feet in length.[3]

While some of the Scythians and Celts went on to become highly civilized and rulers of nations, the nomads among them often became barbarians, going entirely naked and eating raw flesh. Unfortunately, in the process of their association with the Lamanites, the Lamanites apparently took on some of their barbaric natures.

The evil nature of the Lamanites is best described by Enos:

> And I bear record that the people of Nephi did seek diligently to restore the Lamanites unto the true faith in God. But our labors were vain; their hatred was fixed, and they were led by their evil nature that they became wild, and ferocious, and a blood-thirsty people, full of idolatry and filthiness; feeding upon beasts of prey; dwelling in tents, and wandering about in the wilderness with a short skin girdle about their loins and their heads shaven; and their skill was in the bow, and in the cimeter, and the ax. And many of them did eat nothing save it was raw meat; and they were continually seeking to destroy us. (Enos 1:20)

Now, the Yuchi, another tribe of merchant kings, claim to have been the middleman in trade and commerce throughout the mound-building regions. It is believed they are a satellite of the Maya culture and thus likely a mix of Scythians and Danites who arrived in the southeast from one of the islands ruled by Votan when his island empire vanished beneath the sea. The Yuchi are also said to have ties to India where they came to be known as "White Hindoos," or "children of the sun," after converting to the Hindu religion. Unfortunately, Yuchi monks were intent on converting the locals to their sun-worshiping ways, with their success rate among the Lamanites perhaps noted by their custom of marking themselves in their foreheads with a red mark, a tradition common among the Hindoos (see Alma 3:4).

The Yuchi consider themselves the first nation on earth and carried the original priesthood that was then divided into twelve great tribes, with the Schawano-e acting as the high priests of the Yuchi tribes. Unfortunately, the Schawano-e are also identified with the Jaguar Priesthood, those frequently called the Shawnee Indians.[4] The Shawnee, a branch of the Algonquin language family, claim to have formed a confederacy with the Yuchi, and the Shawnee acted as the Levites among the other tribes. It was the consensus among those who explored the mound-building regions in the eighteenth century that during that ancient time there was a powerful confederacy in the area made up closely allied tribes who occupied the valley of the Ohio.

One affiliated tribe appears to have been the Cherokee. Barbara Mann, an instructor at the University of Toledo in African-American and Native American History, maintained that the Cherokees were numbered among the Mound Builders long before they occupied the Appalachian Mountains. While earlier studies found little evidence to connect the Cherokee to the Hopewell, the recent studies of the distribution of mitochondrial DNA lineages among Native American tribes of Northeastern North America by Ripan S. Malhi, Beth A. Schultz, David G. Smith show genetic evidence of a Cherokee intrusion into the southeast, which conforms with Cherokee oral traditions which say their ancestors were builders of the Hopewell earth mounds in the Ohio Valley two thousand years ago. Further, they believe it is possible the populations of the Hopewell culture were descendants of the Proto-Algonquins and that the Cherokee were ultimately displaced into the southeastern United States by the Hopewell from the lower Great Lakes and Ontario once they moved south into Ohio.

While their Nephite brothers were continually moving north, the Lamanites in the land of Nephi (in southwestern New York) moved south along the Allegheny River, and from there ultimately into Ohio. Those who settled along the Allegheny River referred to themselves as the Allegewi, after the river, also Telegwi, or Tallegwi[5] (later changed to Cherokee). While the Lamanites were generally known as warlike men, prone to wickedness and mayhem, many of them were righteous at times. In fact, sometimes the Lamanites proved to be more righteous than the Nephites. Many were converted during various missionary excursions into Lamanite territory. Alma claimed that "as many of the Lamanites as believed in their preaching, and were converted unto the Lord, never did fall away. For they became a righteous people; . . . that they did not fight against God any more, neither against any of their brethren" (Alma 23:5).

A young Irishman named James Adair was especially impressed with the Cherokee. He claims they only had one God whom they called Yohewah (Jehovah) who was the head of their state, and thus the Cherokee claim they needed no other king. After documenting their customs, civil policies, history, language, religion, priests, military customs, agricultures, marriage and funeral rites, and their temperaments and manners, Adair found them all to have close affinities with the customs and traits of the Hebrews. Like the Hebrews, the Cherokee had an ark reminiscent of the ark of the covenant which was carried on the back of a brave as they journeyed. They started their year at the first appearance of the new moon of the vernal equinox, according to the ecclesiastical year as outlined by Moses. Thus, although the law of Moses had been fulfilled with the coming of Christ, they nonetheless continued with what they could remember of the law. Adair maintained that the Cherokee were far more civilized than any of the neighboring tribes.

According to Chief Attakullakulla's ceremonial speech to the Cherokee Nation in 1750, the Cherokee traveled to America from the "rising sun," or the east. He claims they traveled back and forth to Mexico twice over the centuries, making Tennessee, West Virginia, North and South Carolina, and Georgia their home the second time around. From their *Legend of Keetoowah*, we learn they also lived on an island in the Caribbean at one time. They say that God gave them mysterious powers and placed the Cherokee in large settlements on an island located off the coast of South America. It is said that once they arrived, seventy tribes attacked them. But when one of the attackers looked out over their camp from the top of a mountain, he noticed an eagle holding arrows in his claws in the haze of the smoke that rose from their village below. When the warrior told his followers, they ceased their attacks, claiming these were God's people and that if they attacked, they would be destroyed. Yes, indeed, these were God's people, children of Jacob through that Joseph who was sold into Egypt—a detached tribe of the Iroquois.

As the *Legend of Keetoowah* continues, we learn that some of the wise men among them became corrupt. Their wise men were misusing the powers God gave them. Thus, God instructed the more righteous to leave the island, which they did, just before the island began to shake and the tops of the mountains opened up and spewed forth ash in a terrible volcanic eruption. Seven groups set sail to assure their survival. While some likely sailed west to

Central or South America, the Cherokee claim some made it as far away as India and Asia. From there we can suppose they traveled to the Pacific as well. Others simply moved back to North America, the land of their fathers, leaving the wise men behind on the island to die in a cataclysm that left their island sunk beneath the sea. One group settled in the great Smoky Mountain range of what is now North Carolina, Virginia, West Virginia, and eastern Tennessee. A branch who settled in South Carolina, Georgia, and Alabama, were called the Tuscarora. It was here in the mountains they officially became known as Cherokee, although they prefer to call themselves the Tsalagi, or Allegewi, their own name for the Cherokee Nation. A second group settled in New England, where they merged with another exiled Cherokee group to become the Oneida, while a third group settled in what has become Nova Scotia to become the Naskapi. They claim that God was mindful of those in North America and gave them wisdom and guided them.

Part Seven

The Time of Christ

⤳ **19** ⤳

Prelude to Christ

While the philosophies of the Order of Nehor swept through Lamanite territory—where it had all too much success in turning their hearts from God in the century before Christ—the four sons of king Mosiah, Ammon, Aaron, Omner and Himni, had more than just a little success in reintroducing them to the God of their fathers and his son, Jesus Christ. Lehi and Nephi, the two sons of Helaman, also went about doing missionary work, and through their teachings and accompanying trials, succeeded in converting thousands of Lamanites (see Helaman 5:19). During one episode, the conversion of three hundred led to the conversion of thousands more. While it began with the Lamanites casting the Lehi and Nephi into prison, the outcome of their imprisonment was far different than the Lamanites first intended. The Lord encircled Lehi and Nephi with fire to prevent the Lamanites from harming them. As a further deterrent, the earth shook and a dark mist appeared. And then, as if in a whisper, the Lord spoke.

> And it came to pass that there came a voice as if it were above
> the cloud of darkness, saying: Repent ye, repent ye, and seek
> no more to destroy my servants whom I have sent unto you
> to declare good tidings.
>
> And it came to pass when they heard this voice, and
> beheld that it was not a voice of thunder, neither was it a
> voice of a great tumultuous noise, but behold, it was a still
> voice of perfect mildness, as if it had been a whisper, and it
> did pierce even to the very soul. (Helaman 5:29–30)

After calling them to repentance, the voice of the Lord called
again, instructing them that the time was at hand for the Lord of
hosts to walk among men—Christianity and a new age of enlightenment was about to come forth.

> And behold the voice came again, saying: Repent ye, repent
> ye, for the kingdom of heaven is at hand; and seek no more
> to destroy my servants. And it came to pass that the earth
> shook again, and the walls trembled. (Helaman 5:32)

As their call to repentance continued, the Lamanites saw Lehi
and Nephi in the midst of the swirling fires speaking with angels.
Then, as a grand finale:

> And it came to pass that when they cast their eyes about,
> and saw that the cloud of darkness was dispersed from over-
> shadowing them, behold, they saw that they were encircled
> about, yea every soul, by a pillar of fire.
>
> And Nephi and Lehi were in the midst of them; yea,
> they were encircled about; yea, they were as if in the midst of
> a flaming fire, yet it did harm them not, neither did it take
> hold upon the walls of the prison; and they were filled with
> that joy which is unspeakable and full of glory.
>
> And behold, the Holy Spirit of God did come down from
> heaven, and did enter into their hearts, and they were filled as
> if with fire, and they could speak forth marvelous words.
>
> And it came to pass that there came a voice unto them,
> yea, a pleasant voice, as if it were a whisper, saying:

Peace, peace be unto you, because of your faith in my Well Beloved, who was from the foundation of the world.

And now, when they heard this they cast up their eyes as if to behold from whence the voice came; and behold, they saw the heavens open; and angels came down out of heaven and ministered unto them. (Helaman 5:43–48)

So glorious were the events of that day that three hundred Lamanites were converted on the spot, and then they went about converting their brothers. For the most part, the Lamanites hated the Nephites because they had been taught by their fathers to hate them. But, once converted, the Lamanites were every bit as faithful as the Nephites, and often even more so. While the Nephites seemed to bend in the wind with every new doctrine or temptation, the Lamanites stood steadfast in the faith to the point of laying down their lives rather than shed blood again. In time, the Lord removed the curse that had been placed on their forefathers for their wicked behavior, and they became white again. This miraculous transformation was one of the most significant changes to take place among the descendants of Lehi since they first arrived in the promised land nearly six hundred years earlier.

And their curse was taken from them, and their skin became white like unto the Nephites;

And their young men and their daughters became exceedingly fair, and they were numbered among the Nephites, and were called Nephites. And thus ended the thirteenth year. (3 Nephi 2:14–16)

For the first time, many Lamanites set aside their hatred for their white brothers and joined them—even to becoming Nephites themselves. Just as John the Baptist paved the way for the Son of God's appearance among the Jews in the Old World, the efforts of such men as Lehi and Nephi, and an impressive number of

Lamanite missionaries, prepared the unbelieving in their own lands for Christianity.

The years leading up to the visit of Christ was also a time of cleansing. Corruption swept across the land as Satan did his best to bind the righteous before the Savior and his message of hope and salvation arrived. And, as usual, Satan used his most trusted servants to do his dirty work—the Gadianton Robbers. The secret oaths and covenants of the Gadianton were first introduced to Cain by their author, Satan, who introduced it to every generation thereafter.

> And behold, it is he who is the author of all sin. And behold, he doth carry on his works of darkness and secret murder, and doth hand down their plots, and their oaths, and their covenants, and their plans of awful wickedness, from generation to generation according as he can get hold upon the hearts of the children of men. (Helaman 6:28–30)

In teaching his son Helaman, Alma explains that the Jaredites were destroyed because they did not keep God's decree of the land—all who lived within its borders must not only worship him but also must never allow the secret works of darkness to take root. In fact, these secret oaths and covenants were such a threat to the people that Helaman was commanded to keep their works of darkness hidden.

> And now, my son, I command you that ye retain all their oaths, and their covenants, and their agreements in their secret abominations; yea, and all their signs and their wonders ye shall keep from this people, that they know them not, lest peradventure they should fall into darkness also and be destroyed.
>
> For behold, there is a curse upon all this land, that destruction shall come upon all those workers of darkness, according to the power of God, when they are fully ripe; therefore I desire that this people might not be destroyed. (Alma 37:27–29)

Although the secret oaths were hidden, Satan is not bound by such trivial matters and simply reintroduced it to some of the more wicked among the Nephites and Lamanites. As each band of Gadiantons rose in power, the righteous fought against them, although usually failing in the attempt. However, one time, the newly converted Lamanites found unexpected success by converting their enemies rather than kill them (see Helaman 6:37). Nephite dissenters, on the other hand, lured by the secret oaths that promised great wealth and glory, sought the Gadiantons out and joined their wicked bands. In fact, so many joined that in time the righteous were enticed to join their numbers. The Gadiantons even infiltrated the government and brought such disorder that the Nephites began to war among themselves, totally giving themselves over to bloodshed and mayhem.

Prophets like Nephi, the son of Helaman, cried repentance to this people. Unfortunately, by this time Satan had such a firm hold on their hearts that Helaman's efforts were overwhelmingly rejected. He was even rejected in the land north, where he hoped to have better success. When he returned to Zarahemla, he was swept away in sorrow—not for himself, but for his people. Yet, however weak his success had been among his countrymen, in recognition of his unwavering faith and efforts to save his people, the Lord blessed him with the sealing powers (see Helaman 10:4–5). With that added help, Nephi proved to be one of the greatest prophets of his time, being transported by the Spirit from congregation to congregation until everyone had heard the message of Christ.

Other prophets also came into the land to preach repentance—one of the most noteworthy was a Lamanite prophet named Samuel, who spoke to them of many things, including the coming Messiah. He not only prophesied about the signs and wonders that would precede the Savior's birth but also of the devastation that would take place at the time of his death. He explained it was through Christ's death that salvation would come and that those who believed on his name and repented would have their sins remitted. He taught more about the resurrection and explained that Christ would also die to bring about the resurrection of the dead "that thereby man might be brought into the presence of the Lord" (Helaman 14:15). He then spoke of the signs that would accompany the Savior's death (see Helaman 14:21–28).

Many were converted after hearing Samuel's powerful message and were baptized. Satan was not willing to relinquish this congregation yet and thus sent some of his own emissaries to convince them not to believe. Then, in the ninetieth year of the judges, the signs and wonders began to be fulfilled. Angels appeared to men, and wise men declared tidings of great joy. The scriptures began to be fulfilled. In spite of such marvelous manifestations, however, the majority of the people refused to believe and threatened the believers with death if the prophesied star did not arrive by a certain date. So Nephi pled with the Lord for the deliverance of his people. The Lord responded.

> Lift up your head and be of good cheer; for behold, the time is at hand, and on this night shall the sign be given, and on the morrow come I into the world, to show unto the world that I will fulfil all that which I have caused to be spoken by the mouth of my holy prophets. . . .
>
> And behold, the time is at hand, and this night shall the sign be given.
>
> And it came to pass that the words which came unto Nephi were fulfilled, according as they had been spoken; for behold, at the going down of the sun there was no darkness; and the people began to be astonished because there was no darkness when the night came (3 Nephi 1:13–15).

Just as he said, with the going down of the sun, there was no darkness. Moreover, it was light as if it were noon-day. Then a new star arose, and the people knew it was the day the Lord should arrive.

When that tactic did not work, Satan used the Gadiantons in hopes of leading this flock "carefully down to hell" (2 Nephi 28:21). As time progressed, things went from bad to worse, with the Gadiantons repeatedly coming against the Nephites. After several episodes too numerous to mention, the Nephites finally defeated the Gadiantons. However, the Nephites in Zarahemla only knew peace for a short time before Satan began to stir them up to do all manner of iniquity again—this time enticing them to seek power, riches, and vain things of the world. By AD 30, the Nephites were in a state of awful wickedness.

Satan's next plan was to raise up an anti-Christ whose mission would be to convince the Nephites there was no God, and no reason to look forward to Christ—the same scenario that will arise with a latter-day anti-Christ who will attempt to rule the world. We may never know what brought about such a drastic change, but within just a few short years, almost all the righteous had succumbed to sin.

Fortunately, while the various tribes were in many instances enemies, they were all united in their hatred of the Gadianton robbers who had destroyed their government, and thus the tribes united against them (see 3 Nephi 7:12–13). Peace and prosperity followed, but Satan was not yet willing to concede defeat in this ongoing battle between good and evil, and he decided to use the tribes' own prosperity against them. Once he succeeded in creating class distinctions, with those who had the greatest power and wealth thinking themselves better than those who had little, he tempted them into every evil he could conjure up. Tragically, his success rate was staggering. The time was drawing near for the Lord to step in and cleanse the vineyard before his visit to the Nephites.

∼ 20 ∼

The Great Destruction

Once the Christ child was born, Satan conjured up every evil he could think of to lead the Nephites into wickedness and thus seal this flock his while he still had a chance, for the Lord would soon walk among them. Tragically, all too many of the Nephites forsook the God of their fathers and became a decadent and sinful people. Thus, when the Lord's earthly life was finished and he had paid the price for the sins of the world, a great destruction was sent upon the wicked in this part of his vineyard in preparation for his visit to the more faithful. Satan had already sealed many of both the Nephites and Mulekites his, but he would not win them all.

The scriptures tell us that the mighty hand of chastisement came down upon the unrepentant in the form of a terrible tempest and an earthquake. City after city was destroyed; some were carried away in

Crucifixion

157

terrible whirlwinds, while others sunk beneath the sea. Still others were buried beneath mountains; others caught fire after which a dark mist fell upon the region that lasted for three days. This was not a good time for the wicked—but a whole new era of enlightenment and peace was about to dawn for the righteous.

According to the Bible, the sun refused to shine in Jerusalem for three full hours at the time of the Savior's death. "Now from the sixth hour there was darkness over all the land unto the ninth hour" (Matthew 27:45). While three hours of darkness was a sign of the death of the Savior in the Old World, the Prophet Zenos said that those of the isles of the sea would experience three *full* days of darkness, not just three hours, with the greatest isle of all being America. Most of the Eurasian populations of antiquity thought the Old World was the only populated landmass on earth. They thought the mysterious lands across the sea were islands. The Algonquin descendants of Nephi still speak of North America as Turtle Island.

Jacob, the brother of Nephi, explained:

And now, my beloved brethren, seeing that our merciful God has given us so great knowledge concerning these things, let us remember him, and lay aside our sins, and not hang down our heads, for we are not cast off; nevertheless, we have been driven out of the land of our inheritance; but we have been led to a better land, for the Lord has made the sea our path, and we are upon an isle of the sea. (2 Nephi 10:20)

Only the children of Israel made the connection between the three days of darkness that would accompany the Savior's death and the three days of darkness that fell over Egypt in the Lord's efforts to release Israel after four hundred years of bondage to Pharaoh.

And the Lord said unto Moses, Stretch out thine hand toward heaven, that there may be darkness over the land of Egypt, even darkness which may be felt. And Moses stretched forth his hand toward heaven; and there was a thick darkness in all the land of Egypt three days. (Exodus 10:21–22; see also 1 Nephi 19:10)

The Prophet, Samuel spoke to them about this time of darkness, saying the land would remain dark for three days until the Lord rose from the dead.

But behold, as I said unto you concerning another sign, a sign of his death, behold, in that day that he shall suffer death the sun shall be darkened and refuse to give his light unto you; and also the moon and the stars; and there shall be no light upon the face of this land, even from the time that he shall suffer death, for the space of three days, to the time that he shall rise again from the dead. (Helaman 14:20)

That prophecy remained in the minds of the Nephites as they awaited the fulfillment of the prophesied signs and wonders. Although the signs of Christ's coming were eventful, nothing prepared them for the devastation that hit the area when the Savior's earthy mission was complete. The whole world would feel the earth's anguish as she mourned the death of her creator. Half way around the world, the Nephites also felt her suffering; violent quaking resulted in the death of untold thousands. To make matters worse, it was accompanied by a tempest of biblical proportions that lasted three agonizing hours. The very elements mourned.

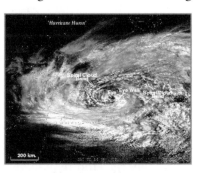

Hurricane Huron

And it came to pass . . . there arose a great storm, such an one as never had been known in all the land.

And there was also a great and terrible tempest; and

there was terrible thunder, insomuch that it did shake the whole earth as if it was about to divide asunder.

And there were exceedingly sharp lightnings, such as never had been known in all the land.

And the city of Zarahemla did take fire.

And the city of Moroni did sink into the depths of the sea, and the inhabitants thereof were drowned.

And the earth was carried up upon the city of Moronihah that in the place of the city there became a great mountain.

And there was a great and terrible destruction in the land southward. (3 Nephi 8:5–11)

Along with the thunderstorm, a tempest was also noted, or a violent windstorm, one that closely parallels a storm which hit Ontario in 1996—a combined hurricane/cyclone. It seems that in addition to the eye of the hurricane, as convective clouds formed, the eye of a tropical cyclone also formed with two centers, one at the east end of Lake Huron and the other to the north of Lake Ontario. The combined force of an earthquake and a hurricane/cyclone no doubt caused tsunami-type waves in the greater lakes that we can suppose swept away entire lakeside villages. Thus, one can see why there was more destruction in the land northward, which took the brunt of the storm, although the land south took a pretty hard hit as well (3 Nephi 8:12).

Those who were spared no doubt cried out to God for deliverance, a prayer that was finally answered after three hours of terror. Even then, the land remained in darkness.

And it came to pass that when the thunderings, and the lightnings, and the storm, and the tempest, and the quakings of the earth did cease, for behold, they did last for about the space of three hours; and it was said by some that the time was greater; nevertheless, all these great and terrible things were done in about the space of three hours and then behold, there was darkness upon the face of the land. (3 Nephi 8:19)

The Nephites could hardly see their hands before their faces so thick was the darkness. A palpable vapor of dense, dark fog hovered for the next three days, blotting out the sun and the moon and the stars.

> And it came to pass that there was thick darkness upon all the face of the land, insomuch that the inhabitants thereof who had not fallen could feel the vapor of darkness;
>
> And there could be no light, because of the darkness, neither candles, neither torches; neither could there be fire kindled with their fine and exceedingly dry wood, so that there could not be any light at all;
>
> And there was not any light seen, neither fire, nor glimmer, neither the sun, nor the moon, nor the stars, for so great were the mists of darkness which were upon the face of the land.
>
> And it came to pass that it did last for the space of three days that there was no light seen; and there was great mourning and howling and weeping among all the people continually; yea, great were the groanings of the people, because of the darkness and the great destruction which had come upon them (3 Nephi 8:20–23).

When the wrath of God finally came down upon the Gadiantons, fire is mentioned rather than a tempest. While the fire that destroyed the city of Zarahemla could well be attributed to a lightning strike, no mention of a tempest is made when describing the destruction of Gadianton cities. What kind of fire that was used to destroy these cities has not been revealed—perhaps it was the impact of some celestial orb, or maybe the eruption of a volcano. Canada has nearly every type volcano found on earth that are responsible for many of Canada's geographical features and mineral deposits. Although most are in the west, the Mackenzi dike swarm, which form the roots of a volcanic province, is the largest dike swarm in the world. It stretches across Canada from the Arctic

Volcano and lightning

to the Great Lakes. A huge extinct caldera lay just to the north of Lake Superior, with another huge crater found in New Hampshire. Scott Fitzpatrick explains that the Ossipee Mountains in New Hampshire are the best examples of a ring dike formation in the world, located at the center of an ancient volcanic crater.

Quebec's Monteregian Hills are still another group of extinct volcanoes. They consist of a series of eight butte-type mountains located about fifty miles from Montreal and stretch across the Saint Lawrence River to the Appalachian highlands. They are the eroded remnants of the oldest volcanoes in the New England hot spot track that extends along the ocean floor to underwater volcanoes off the coast of Africa.

While most of the volcanic activity noted in the region is thought to have taken place millions of years ago, the traditions of the American Indians tell a different story, as does an eyewitness to an eruption somewhere along the Saint Lawrence River in the late 1800s. The traditions of the American Indians speak of a "fire mountain" in either Quebec or Labrador, which was active until at least a few centuries ago. Some of the accounts noted by early settlers along the Saint Lawrence River noted earthquakes, followed by periods of profound darkness, violent gusts of winds, rain, and lightning, just as described in the scriptures. Who is to say something similar did not take place during the days of the Book of Mormon, only much worse.

Wherever the fire came from, a hot spot eruption or fragments of some comet or asteroid, or simply by the command of God, a number of Gadianton cities were completely destroyed at the same time the people in Zarahemla were experiencing the worst storm of their lives (see 3 Nephi 9:9–12.) It is hard to imagine the destruction that must have hit the region at the time of the Savior's death. The scriptures say that not only did a major tornado-producing storm hit the region, but an earthquake, and quite possibly a volcanic eruption whose plumes of smoke and ash darkened the sky until the third day when the Savior rose from the tomb. What a traumatic event the three days of terror and destruction must have been for the Nephites. Death and destruction were everywhere; friends, neighbors, relatives had been taken home to God to wait an awful judgment, and the land was torn up from one end to the other. And to top it off, the voice of the Savior had spoken to them from out of heaven as one man speaks to another, not in a dream, nor vision, but an audible voice—how were they to absorb it all?

The voice of the Lord speaking from out of the darkness said:

> Wo, wo, wo unto this people; wo unto the inhabitants of the whole earth except they shall repent; for the devil laugheth, and his angels rejoice, because of the slain of the fair sons and daughters of my people; and it is because of their iniquity and abominations that they are fallen! (3 Nephi 9:2)

— 21 —

The Time of Christ

After the tragic yet wonderfully grand event of Christ's death and resurrection, Jesus appeared to his disciples in Jerusalem off and on for the next forty days before giving the kingdom over to the twelve saying, "All power is given unto me in heaven and in earth. Go ye therefore, and teach all nations, baptizing them in the name of the Father, and of the Son, and of the Holy Ghost" (Matthew 28:18–19.) This they did but not before making an impact on their own countrymen. In fact, along with the twelve, Stephen took up the cause and defied the Sadducees by preaching of the risen Lord throughout Jerusalem, and Luke claimed the number of converts reached the spectacular number of three to five thousand daily.

Not only were the Twelve Apostles commanded to preach to the world, but other prophets were also admonished to teach of him. King Benjamin, a Nephite ruler in the New World a century before Christ, said the Lord sent many prophets among the nations of the world—even before his birth:

And the Lord God hath sent his holy prophets among all the children of men, to declare these things to every kindred, nation, and tongue, that thereby whosoever should believe that Christ should come, the same might receive remission of their sins, and rejoice with exceedingly great joy, even as though he had already come among them (Mosiah 3:13).

While we do not yet have a record of the Nephites who went about preaching of the risen Lord, it is said that of the Old World apostles, Andrew went to Macedonia, Greece, Scythia, Asia Minor, and Russia. Bartholomew went mainly to India and Armenia. James preached in Persia and Spain. John traveled to Palestine and Asia Minor; Judas to Mesopotamia and Persia; Matthew to Egypt and Ethiopia; Philip to France, Southern Russia, and Asia Minor; Peter to Pontius, Galatia, Bithrynia, Cappadocia and Asia; and Simon Zelotes to Egypt, Mauritania, Africa, Libya, and Britain. Thomas preached in India and to the Parthians, Medes, and Persians, with some writers claiming he also made it to China and to the Americas. Dr. John Matthew Thekkel claimed Thomas reached Kerala in India just twenty years after Christ's crucifixion. There he settled in Malabar and then expanded his missionary work to China. Thekkel claims further that he "was martyred in Tamil Nadu on his return to India in AD 72 and was buried in Mylapore near Madras."[1] Some say he even made it to the Americas, a part of the world not yet visited by the other apostles.

We have little to go on in reconciling obscure legends of white, bearded prophets said to have walked the Americas around the first century, but the Book of Mormon does provide the most amazing documented account of the Savior's visit to any company of men after his death and resurrection. The Savior's appearance to his faithful flock near the temple in Bountiful was so glorious that words alone cannot express the grandeur of the occasion, as the Father announced his Son.

And it came to pass that while they were thus conversing one with another, they heard a voice as if it came out of heaven; and they cast their eyes round about, for they understood not the voice which they heard; and it was not a harsh voice, neither was it a loud voice; never-

Christ

theless, and notwithstanding it being a small voice it did pierce them that did hear to the center, insomuch that there was no part of their frame that it did not cause to quake; yea, it did pierce them to the very soul, and did cause their hearts to burn.

And it came to pass that again they heard the voice, and they understood it not.

And again the third time they did hear the voice, and did open their ears to hear it; and their eyes were towards the sound thereof; and they did look steadfastly towards heaven, from whence the sound came.

And behold, the third time they did understand the voice which they heard; and it said unto them:

Behold my Beloved Son, in whom I am well pleased, in whom I have glorified my name—hear ye him (3 Nephi 11:1–7).

After hearing that glorious announcement, the stunned crowd watched as the Savior descended and stood in their midst. Then, after complying with his directive to step forward and feel the wounds in his hands and feet, the people fell to the ground and worshipped him. Only then did the Savior announce his Godhood. He said:

Behold, I am Jesus Christ, whom the prophets testified shall come into the world.

And behold, I am the light and the life of the world; and I have drunk out of that bitter cup which the Father hath given me, and have glorified the Father in taking upon me

the sins of the world, in the which I have suffered the will of the Father in all things from the beginning (3 Nephi 11:10–11).

The Lord then taught and blessed them, and organized his Church among them.

The eye hath never seen, neither hath the ear heard, before, so great and marvelous things as we saw and heard Jesus speak unto the Father;

And no tongue can speak, neither can there be written by any man, neither can the hearts of men conceive so great and marvelous things as we both saw and heard Jesus speak; and no one can conceive of the joy which filled our souls at the time we heard him pray for us unto the Father. . . .

And they arose from the earth, and he said unto them: Blessed are ye because of your faith. And now behold, my joy is full.

And when he had said these words, he wept, and the multitude bare record of it, and he took their little children, one by one, and blessed them, and prayed unto the Father for them.

And when he had done this he wept again (3 Nephi 17:16–25).

Legends that give veiled references to Christ's visit to other nations pale in comparison, for the Book of Mormon claims that not only did Jesus appear, but angels were also present. Fire encircled their little ones as angels ministered to them, and numerous others were also blessed and healed. The scriptures say he ordained twelve disciples and instructed them in every aspect of religious government, and even provided the name whereby his church and its members should be known—by *his* name, for it is his church, and should be named after him and no one else.

Stories of walking prophets have been documented in various parts of the New World, many of which were collected by L. Taylor Hansen in her impressive book, *He walked the Americas*. But one prophet in particular seems worth mentioning, a green-eyed man referred to as Kate Zahl, who instructed those he was teaching to name him anything they liked, for names meant nothing to him. Hence, the people in each region knew him by a different name. However, we might remember that the first thing the resurrected Lord said upon greeting the Nephites in Bountiful was "Behold, I am Jesus Christ, whom the prophets testified shall come into the world" (3 Nephi 11:10). How were they to have recognized their Savior if they knew him by another name? The name of Jesus Christ is the very name we covenant to remember in the sacrament prayer—a name that has been an integral part of his identity from the beginning of time and will continue to be throughout the eternities. Of equal importance, it will be by his name and none other that salvation will come to the children of man.

> And moreover, I say unto you, that there shall be no other name given nor any other way nor means whereby salvation can come unto the children of men, only in and through the name of Christ, the Lord Omnipotent (Mosiah 3:17).

After announcing his godhood to his Nephite flock, Jesus then walked among them and healed them just as he had done in the Old World. He blessed their children and organized his Church among them. His prayers were so wondrous they could not be repeated. He gave instructions on daily living similar to the Beatitudes and commanded them to baptize in his name—except little children who were exempt from that ordinance until the age of accountability, because they are innocent and naturally saved by virtue of his Atonement.

Christ also predicted the future. He told of the rise of a free people in the land of promise and of the coming forth of the Book of Mormon. He foretold the rise of the New Jerusalem, the gathering of Israel, and the return of the tribes who have been lost. He told of the last days when nations would be in distress and the righteous gathered to Zion, and of his ultimate return to save the righteous and to burn the wicked. In fact, he expounded all things from the beginning to the end—things that could not be written.

In the account of Christ's visit to his faithful Saints in Bountiful, the Savior made it clear that he fully intended to visit others of his lost flock. We first hear of his intentions of visiting others of the house of Israel while he was still in Jerusalem. He said:

> And other sheep I have, which are not of this fold: them also
> I must bring, and they shall hear my voice; and there shall be
> one fold, and one shepherd (John 10:16).

After making himself known to those of Lehi's seed in Bountiful, he said:

> And verily I say unto you, that ye are they of whom I said: Other
> sheep I have which are not of this fold; them also I must bring, and they
> shall hear my voice; and there shall be one fold, and one shepherd. (3
> Nephi 15:21)

> Although the God of the entire world, the Lord's mission
> was to the house of Israel. It was foreordained that the gen-
> tile nations would be converted by the power of the Holy
> Ghost and not through the physical senses alone. Therefore,
> they would be blessed beyond measure, for those converted
> by the spirit are more deeply converted than those who rely

on the senses of sight or sound, as was aptly demonstrated by the Jews who both saw and heard the Savior yet felt obliged to crucify him.

And they understood me not that I said they shall hear my voice; and they understood me not that the Gentiles should not at any time hear my voice—that I should not manifest myself unto them save it were by the Holy Ghost. (3 Nephi: 15:23)

The episode of the Savior's visit to the faithful in Bountiful itself was such a glorious experience that for the first time since their fathers first entered the promised land, the people throughout the northeast and their trading partners from far and wide enjoyed a time of peace. Moreover, with the destruction of the more wicked, the Nephites could now mingle freely with the Lamanites.

Prophets during that time began major missionary excursions throughout the land. They were given the power to heal the sick, cast out devils, teach and preach, and to baptize. They also had the gift of tongues, which allowed them to teach in various nations. They were all priestly men, some of which had the sealing powers that gave them the ability to command the elements. Thus, it was a glorious time to have lived in the promised land.

—୬ 22 ୬—

The Post-Christian Decline

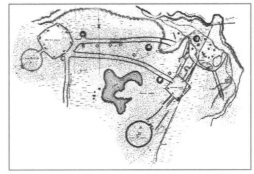

We learn from the Book of Mormon that the first century following the Savior's visit to Bountiful was a time of peace and mutual fellowship (see 4 Nephi 1:3). Yet, while Satan was bound for a time, peace was not destined to go on indefinitely. A century and a half later, a new type architecture showed up in the Ohio Valley, and thus a new people, for the architecture was so different from the earlier structures that Kennedy thinks they must have been built by a "cadre of priestly architect/astronomers—geomancers—who brought new ways of building as distinct from the old as the Gothic was from the Romanesque."[1] A consensus is now

Newark Works, Licking County, Ohio
Squire & Davis, 1937

formed that these structures were built in the central region of North America as early as the time of Christ.[2] Kennedy found no evidence to suggest the squaring of their earthworks began before AD 150, however. So we can assume it was around this time the new architects arrived on the scene.

Many archaeologists have noticed the similarities between these earthworks and those in the British Isles where the Druids were well-known as astronomers and necromancers and for their geometric designed earthworks. Several ancient writers mentioned the Druid's use of geometry in their various works, including Pomponius Mela, who claimed the Druids were "conversant with the most sublime speculations in geometry and in measuring the magnitude of the earth."[3] It would appear that a certain number of Druid astronomer-priests from England may have made it successfully to America in the century or two after Christ. Unfortunately, these astronomer-priests may have had a negative affect on the Hopewell, notwithstanding the fact that they may have been recently converted Christians.

While the Druidic Order remains somewhat mysterious, some insist that the Druids in England practiced a less corrupted version than what was introduced into Ireland by the Tuatha de Danaan, whose magic arts came from an emissary of the devil himself. In England, the standards fostered by the brotherhood were so lofty that it was the official religion of England until the advent of Christianity. From then on the Druids were referred to as Culdee, a name supposedly referring to the Judean refugees, or "strangers," who found refuge in Britain in AD 37 and brought with them the Christian faith. It is said that the Druids were the first to be converted to the new religion because of the remarkable similarities between the two faiths and they became some of the most faithful missionaries in the world. The Druid's name for God before the introduction of Christianity included terms such as "The Mysterious One," "The Wonderful," or "The Ancient of Days"[4]—all old Testament terms.

In spite of the rapid conversion of the Druids in England to Christianity, Isabel Elders, quoting Spence, said:

> "There are many circumstances," writes Lewis Spence, "connected with the Culdees to show that if they practiced a species of Christianity their doctrine still retained a large measure of the Druidic philosophy, and that indeed they were the direct descendants of the Druidic caste. . . . The Culdees . . . were Christianized Druids, mingling with their faith a large element of the ancient Duridic cultus. . . . But all their power they ascribed to Christ—Christ is my Druid, said Columba."[5]

Once the Druids in the British Isles were converted, their universities were turned into Christian colleges and Druid priests were turned into Christian ministers, many of which were sent out into the world to spread the word of God. More left their homeland as they fled Roman persecution, and many made their way to Ireland and to Wales, which were not yet under Roman rule. From there it can be supposed that some sailed west to America from ports unguarded by Roman legions in hopes of finding refuge and a place they could practice their new religion in peace. Unfortunately, it would appear that those who began a new wave of construction in Ohio were among those who still clung to the old ways of the Druidic order, which caused friction between the new Druid refugees and those who followed the true ways of Christ.

Time was also proving to be an enemy, for the tales of the Savior's visit to various parts of his vineyard were quickly fading, and people began to fall into apostasy—including those in Zarahemla. In prophesying about the time of Christ's visit to the faithful in Bountiful and the decline which followed, Jacob, the brother of Nephi, said, "But

Ansgar the missionary preaching Christianity to the heathen Swedes
Hugo Hamilton, 1830

the Son of Righteousness shall appear unto them; and he shall heal them, and they shall have peace with him, until three generations shall have passed away" (2 Nephi 26:9–10).

Ritchie believes that somewhere either shortly before or after AD 160, small break-off groups from the major Hopewell centers in the Ohio River Valley fused with the Point Peninsula populations in New York to produce a mixed culture that he refers to as the Squawkie Hill phase. It was his belief that to "varying degrees" the existing social groups (of Nephites) were "suffused with Hopewellian religious ideas, practices and material cultural elements, some of which were doubtless cult-related."[6]

His version varies little from what we learn in the scriptures, which tell us that by AD 201. new churches began to spread through the land, and for the next ten years spread like wildfire. While they make it clear that the new churches were Christian, they nonetheless denied much of the doctrines of Christ, just as many of the newly converted Druids were quickly spreading across the Ohio Valley and apparently penetrating Zarahemla.

> And it came to pass that when two hundred and ten years had passed away there were many churches in the land; yea, there were many churches which professed to know the Christ, and yet they did deny the more parts of his gospel, insomuch that they did receive all manner of wickedness, and did administer that which was sacred unto him to whom it had been forbidden because of unworthiness. (4 Nephi 1:27)

A second church mentioned in this era did not even believe in Christ and persecuted those who did.

> And again, there was another church which denied the Christ; and they did persecute the true church of Christ, because of their humility and their belief in Christ; . . . And they did smite upon the people of Jesus; but the people of Jesus did not smite again. And thus they did dwindle in unbelief and wickedness, from year to year, even until two hundred and thirty years had passed away. (4 Nephi 1:29, 34)

The archaeologist Roger Kennedy was not too far off when he concluded that the native populations ultimately rebelled against their brothers in Ohio, which sent them to the hills around the close of the second century and they began to "fortify their hilltop enclosures."[7]

By the time 244 years had passed away from the time of Christ, more wicked people lived in Zarahemla than the people of God (see 4 Nephi 1:40). The scriptures tell us they continued to build up false churches until 250 years passed away, and then 260 years (see 4 Nephi 1:41). Unfortunately, things continued to go downhill from there, with the addition of astrology and certain occult practices signaling the beginning of the people's downward spiral.

The archaeological evidence suggests the people of the region went from using the priesthood to heal the sick and perform miracles to depending upon Shamans and magicians who used hallucinogenic drugs to produce the state of consciousness they wanted. These magic arts were handed down from generation to generation by the Celtic tribes, practices that were particularly abhorrent to the Nephites, who mentioned such practices when lamenting their various woes: "No man could keep that which was his own, for the thieves, and the robbers, and the murderers, and the magic art, and the witchcraft which was in the land" (Mormon 2:10).

By the time three hundred years had passed away, both the Nephites and Lamanites were equally wicked, for they had once again embraced the secret works of the Gadiantons. The only righteous in the land were the Three Nephites. After 320 years had passed away, Ammoran was constrained by the Holy Spirit to hide up the sacred records of his people (see 4 Nephi 1:48).

Archaeologist Olaf Prufer claims the Hopewell went through "a long and piecemeal degeneration,"[8] which most now agree ended around AD 350—very close to the time the scriptures place the demise of the Nephite nation in AD 384—because all had turned to sin (see Alma 45:10–12).

The scriptures say it was the rising generations who initially fell away, with each generation following until the Nephites were ripe in iniquity. We would have to assume they had finally given in to the decadent ways of the sun-worshipers in the area. They were even practicing human sacrifice, an evil that brought the wrath of God upon the whole area, starting with the Hopewell. And since the Lamanites were proving to be more righteous than the Nephites, the Lord used them to do his purposes.

Arthur C. Parker claims the Cherokee and the Algonquins living around the Great Lakes crowded the mound builders of

The taking of a human heart from a sacrificial victim.

Ohio until, after a long protracted war, they finally overcame them and took control of mound building country, absorbing large numbers of the conquered into their own tribal divisions, likely those of their own kinsmen.

During this period of decline, Prufer noted an end to widespread trade relations, a decline in the building of large mounds and ceremonial enclosures, and an end to the practice of placing large amounts of grave offerings with their burials. Stuart Struever maintains that the end of the Hopewell came around AD 350.[9] when practically all remnants of the great Hopewell culture and its economic and artistic inspiration were abandoned. Their populations returned to the localized tribal way of living that existed before the Hopewell.

The Nephites had completely forgotten the visitation of the Savior, who had walked among their fathers just a few centuries earlier and taught them of their Heavenly Father's kingdom. The Jaredites were the first to lose their place in the promised land because they forgot the Lord, and then the Hopewell had followed the same path, and for the same reason. Many Nephites were among the Hopewell at this time. Those who survived fled south on a long migration that took them to Mexico, fulfilling the Lord's decree that only those who worshipped him would prosper in the promised land, while all others would be swept away.

Part Eight

The Fall

23

The Fall of
the Ohio Hopewell

Once the Lamanites gathered their forces against their Nephite brothers, they decided to go against the Hopewell as well, because the Nahuas among them were preparing for a revolt of their own in hopes of taking control of the entire region. Arthur C. Parker suggests the local warriors (whom he believed to be the Cherokee) moved against the Ohio Hopewell until they finally took control of Hopewell territory, absorbing large numbers of the conquered into their own tribal divisions, likely their own kinsmen. He believed the Cherokee were probably assisted in this conquest by the neighboring Algonquin tribes, who together succeeded in expelling the Hopewell from the land. While the bones of thousands of Nephites have been discovered in burial pits all across New York after their exterminating war with the Lamanites, the large amount of bones one would expect to find of the Hopewell after their fall seem to be missing. It has been assumed that the majority of the Hopewell fled the land rather than a face the possibility of death at the hands of the invading warrior bands or, even worse, subjugation.

Actually, this theory corresponds well with the traditions of the Celtic artisans, referred to as Nahuas, who ultimately became known as Toltecs. It seems that the name Toltec was initially applied to the Nahuas while they were living in a great city called Tlachiacatzin, a city with a numerous population that was renown throughout the region. Apparently, the city was also known as Toltecatl, not only after its founder and leader, but because the city's occupants personified all that the name implied—*Toltec* means artist, craftsmen, or men of great learning. The Toltecs were known for their great abilities and skills in the mechanical arts, and also a number of inventions were attributed to them. Although the city was a Nahua city, all the occupants of the city and the whole nation surrounding it, came to be known as Toltecs because of their skills in the arts of civilized living.

In time, the Nahuas grew to be a mighty nation; in fact, it became so great that two princes among them desired the kingdom for themselves—all of it. The local tribes would have none of it, however, for they considered themselves the supreme lords of the territory, a region many suggest was the empire known as Huehue Tlapalan in the old books of Mexico.

J. D. Baldwin said regarding the exhaustive research of C Brasseur de Bourbourg:

> Previous to the history of the Toltec domination in Mexico, we notice in the annals of the country . . . the existence of an ancient empire known as Huehue-Tlapalan, from which the Toltecs, or Nahuas, came to Mexico in consequence of a revolution or invasion, and from which they had a long and toilsome migration to the Aztec Plateau. He believes that Huehe-Tlapalan was the country of the Mound Builders in the Mississippi and Ohio Valleys; According to the native books he has examined, it was somewhere at a distance in the northeast [1]

The timeline for the start of the rebellion is placed 305 years after the time of Christ, about the time we read in the scriptures about the Gadianton Robbers spreading across the land and into Zarahemla. (Ixtlilxochitl places the revolt in AD 338.)

> And it came to pass that when three hundred years had passed away, both the people of Nephi and the Lamanites had become exceedingly wicked one like unto another.
>
> And it came to pass that the robbers of Gadianton did spread over all the face of the land; and there were none that were righteous save it were the disciples of Jesus. And gold and silver did they lay up in store in abundance, and did traffic in all manner of traffic.
>
> And it came to pass that after three hundred and five years had passed away, (and the people did still remain in wickedness) Amos died; and his brother, Ammaron, did keep the record in his stead. (4 Nephi 1:45–47)

Arriving at a date for the departure of this royal company from Huehue Tlapalan, Ixtlilxochitl proceeds from the time of the earthquake, which he calculates came at the time of the Savior's death, or AD 33.

> Three hundred and five years later, when the empire had been long at peace, two chief descendants of the royal house of the Toltecs, raised a revolt for the purpose of deposing the legitimate successor to the throne. The rebellious chiefs were, after long wars, driven out of their city Tlachicatzin in Huehue Tlapallan, with all their numerous families and allies. They were pursued by their kindred of the city or country . . . for sixty leagues, to a place . . . they named . . . "little Tlapalan" . . . and they were accompanied on their forced migration by five other chiefs. [2]

Not only was the date he gives for the earthquake correctly calculated to have taken place the year the Savior suffered and died (AD 33), but the long period of peace he claims followed the

Jesus Christ

death of the Savior can be reconciled with the two hundred years the scriptures say prevailed in the land after the time of Christ (see 4 Nephi 1:45–47). The scriptures say this golden era of peace was followed by another century of decline, thus making it three hundred years before the people completely gave themselves over to evil again—a date just five years shy of the 305 years Ixtlilxochitl said the revolt began.

Interestingly, the forty-seven year war between the Nephites and the Lamanites, which ended in favor of the Lamanites, began around AD 327 (see 4 Nephi 2:1–3). Not surprisingly, things went downhill from there. By AD 337 war was on the horizon for both the Nephites and Hopewell. Once that time came, Foster claimed there was a terrible struggle, but when the Toltecs were "no longer able to resist successfully, [they] were obliged to abandon their country to escape complete subjugation."[3]

While the Nephites in New York were driven to the Hill Cumorah, where they were exterminated en-mass, the Hopewell fled south toward Mexico. Thus, the Nephites were not the only ones struggling to survive during this terrible time of destruction. The war that claimed the lives of every Nephite man, woman, and child (except Moroni) was apparently a regional war, not just one confined to Nephite territory. The Lamanites wanted all their white brothers gone, not just a few.

We can assume that the Nahuas, or Toltecs, among the Hopewell escaped complete annihilation because, unlike the Nephites, they had not been visited by the Savior. for they were an idolatrous people and of mixed blood, and the Savior's mission was exclusively to the house of Israel. Nonetheless, the Lord

had simply had enough of their
pagan ways, for they were defiling the promised land. So once
when the Lamanites decided to
reclaim the land for themselves,
the Lord allowed them to force the
Hopewell out. After a migration
that took 104 years to complete,

the ousted Nahua/Toltec princes, along with their numerous families and allies, ultimately made their way into Mexico. Although
they would be classed as a Nahua nation there, they would forever
be distinguished as Toltecs. Robert Baldwin said:

> All the accounts say the Toltecs came at different times, by
> land and sea, mostly in small companies, and always from
> the northeast. This can be explained only by supposing
> they came from the sea from the mouth of the Mississippi
> River or from the Gulf Coast near it, and by land through
> Texas. But the country from which they came was invariably
> Huehue Tlapalan.[4]

Interestingly, the R1b DYS19=15 Haplotype #25 exhibits its
highest match frequencies among the Hispanic populations of
Mexico and in Ireland, Italy, and Switzerland, suggesting it might
be of Celtic or Iberian origin.

24

The Fall of Zarahemla

ueled by their success against the Hopewell, the Lamanites gathered their forces and came down upon the Nephites like a great swarm of locust. Because the Lord was no longer with the wicked Nephites, all they could do was gather into their strongholds and fortifications. Unfortunately, the Lamanites just kept coming and coming, pushing them further and further toward the land of Cumorah, where they were ultimately destroyed.

The horrific battle that culminated in the deaths of the Nephites around the Hill Cumorah can be classed among the world's greatest battles.

Battle
by John Olive

The Nephites had been duly warned about their wicked behavior. The high priests and prophets had preached repentance time and time again, but they finally gave up. Their people were so fixated upon sin and bloodshed that nothing would deter them any longer. Even Mormon was forbidden to preach to them anymore, because the Spirit had withdrawn, and no one was listening. Thus, blood and carnage reigned until the land ran red with blood. Swords, daggers, spears, and anything else the Nephites could wield clashed with those of the Lamanites on the plains around Cumorah, until the battle ended and the land fell silent.

The terrible battle that destroyed the last of the Nephite population had been brewing for centuries, and it finally came to a head in AD 384. Only weeks before the land had been teeming with life. Thousands of men, women and children had poured into the regions around the Hill Cumorah, creating an enormous army—one determined to rid the land of the Lamanites, who had been a scourge and a plague to the Nephites from their earliest days in the land. Not only had they taken over most of their territory, but were now slaying every Nephite they came across. Thus, a showdown was imminent.

For four long years those who called themselves Nephites had been gathering in anticipation of one final battle, a battle that, if they won, would mean an end to the Lamanites and a return of their lands. But, if they lost, would mean their own complete destruction. Fueled by pride and a sense of invincibility, the Nephites took the chance. Tragically, those who had such high hopes of victory were soon moldering on the ground. Not a cry was heard—not the rustling of armor or the stumbling steps of survivors, because all were dead. Only the quiet retreat of the Lamanites as they withdrew from that blood-soaked battlefield to recover and rejoice in their victory was heard above the silence. It had been a bloody conflict. Both Nephites and Lamanites

Hill Cumorah

died by the thousands. Their death cries must have echoed across the land from dawn until dusk, stopping only after every Nephite man, woman, and child had been killed—all but a handful. Only then did the Lamanites withdraw.

When the first rays of sunlight appeared, the scriptures tell us the few who survived helped Moroni carry his wounded father up the slopes of the Hill Cumorah to survey the aftermath of the previous day's slaughter. But nothing prepared them for what they saw once they reached the top. It was a scene of indescribable horror that extended in every direction as far as the eye could see. Dead bodies were everywhere. The ten thousand of twenty-three captains lay slain upon the ground beside their wives and children, all heaped up one upon the other and covered with blood—all were dead, never to walk the land again or rejoice in the bounties the Lord gives those who love him and keep his commandments. Instead, they had chosen a darker path and introduced sorcerers and witchcraft into the land. They entertained magic and every diabolical scheme Satan inspired to lead the people away from God. They worshipped idols and turned their faces away from that one true God who had led their forefathers from destruction in Jerusalem. All had turned to sin, and all reveled in it. All that was left was death, because the Lord could no longer stay the mighty hand of retribution.

It must have been all Moroni could do to hold back his

emotions as he gazed in horror over the battlefield and heard his father's heart wrenching cry for the loss of his people.

> O ye fair ones, how could ye have departed from the ways of the Lord!
> O ye fair ones, how could ye have rejected that Jesus, who stood with open arms to receive you!
> Behold, if ye had not done this, ye would not have fallen. But behold, ye are fallen, and I mourn your loss.
> O ye fair sons and daughters, ye fathers and mothers, ye husbands and wives, ye fair ones, how is it that ye could have fallen!
> But behold, ye are gone, and my sorrows cannot bring your return. (Mormon 6:17–19)

The things they witnessed that day were things no man should ever have to see—no, not even God. Yet there they were.

In spite of the tragic end of his people, Moroni still had one more job to complete. He was divinely commissioned to record the events leading up to the final destruction of his people, including their demise. Not surprisingly, Moroni found it nearly impossible to describe the awful depravity that led up to the annihilation of his people. He touched upon it only lightly, daring not to give a full account of the things that he had seen lest the reader at some future time be harrowed up in inconsolable sorrow because of their unspeakable wickedness.

Moroni

Moroni knew why the Lord allowed his brethren to die, but he had not anticipated that he would be the sole survivor—especially after finding his father and a few others alive after the battle ended. He must have thought that if they all banded together they might raise up another faithful pocket of saints. But, sadly, such was not to be the case. It was not long before the survivors all joined the ranks of the dead. He was alone—truly alone—except for those who wanted to destroy him, the Lamanites.

25

Footprints of a Vanished Race

The numerous bone pits discovered in western and central New York are evidence enough that terrible wars once raged across the Cumorah lands—hurriedly dug graves facilitated the burial of hundreds of the dead, even thousands. Moreover, numerous oak fortifications left behind by the Nephites as they made their final stands against the enemy were also found, fortifications exactly like those built in Moroni's day.

Many historians have mentioned the terrible wars and destruction that took place in the land in prehistoric times. O. Turner said:

> We are surrounded by evidence that a race preceded the present Indians, farther advanced in civilization and the arts, and far more numerous. Here and there upon the brow of hills, at the head of ravines, are their fortifications, their location selected with skill and adapted to refuge, subsistence and defense. Uprooted trees of the forest that are the growth of many centuries, expose their molding remains, the uncovered mounds with masses of their skeletons

promiscuously heaped one on top of the other, as if they were the gathered and hurriedly entombed dead of well contested battlefields . . .

Although not confined to this region, there is perhaps no portion of the United States where ancient relics are more numerous. Commencing near Oswego River, they extended westwardly over all the western counties of the state. . . Then as now the western portion of New York state had attractions and inducements to make it a favorite residence of this ancient people, . . . made this their refuge in a war of extermination, . . . That here was war of extermination we may well conclude from masses of human skeletons we find indiscriminately thrown together, indicating a common and simultaneous sepulcher from which age, infancy, sex and no condition, was exempt.[1]

Even people outside the LDS community claim western New York was the place of extinction for an ancient civilization. And those who are familiar with the Book of Mormon will recognize the civilization as being the Nephites, and before them, the Jaredites. In fact, the land itself has spoken, for no other region in the Americas provides more evidence of ancient warfare than western New York.

The museums in New York State are filled with the instruments of warfare that had been fashioned by the red men and so freely used in that historic area. The opinion is expressed in all those relic halls that western New York was the site of an ancient battlefield. There is more evidence of a well planned defensive warfare in that locality than there is in any other region on the American continent. It is the opinion of most scholars that the defenses on the drumlin hills were prepared by a people more civilized than the Indians and were exterminated by the inferior race who were still in possession of the country when Columbus discovered this land.[2]

The hills and valleys of western New York are filled with

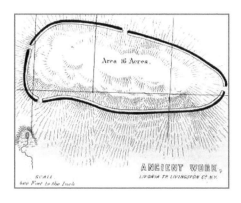

Fortified Site

evidence of ancient warfare. In his research of the region for the Smithsonian Institute, E. G. Squire found hundreds of such fortified sites. More than one thousand sites were found in Ontario, Livingston, Genesee, and Monroe Counties alone, with nearly five hundred sites in Monroe County, and over a one hundred fortified hilltops and strongholds in Genesee County. One large fort in western New York described in the book *The Ruins Revisited* by a historian who simply referred to himself as an *Americanist*, was supposedly capable of enclosing sixty thousand soldiers and their families.

Henry Clyde Shetrone noticed the strategic position of the fortifications that covered so many of western New York's hills, which he noted were often equipped with palisades set into their low earthen walls. He said that the people of this region

> once presented a scene of war, and war in its most horrible form, where blood is the object, and the deficiencies of the field make up by the slaughter of innocence and imbicility. That it was here that a feeble band was collected, "a remnant of mighty battles fought in vain," to make a last effort for the country of their birth, the ashes of their ancestors and the altars of their gods. That the crisis was met with fortitude, and sustained with valor, need not be doubted. . . . But their efforts were vain, and flight or death were the alternatives. [3]

After researching the region, B. H. Roberts said:

> These described fortifications and burial mounds make it clear that central and western New York at some time has

been the scene of destructive battles; and the fact constitutes strong presumptive evidence of the statements of the Book of Mormon that great battles were fought there.[4]

Reflect upon the following experience of the Apostles Brigham Young Jr. and George Q. Cannon as they visited the sacred Hill Cumorah in New York State in 1873 (*Millennial Star*, Aug. 19, 1873).

Undoubtedly great changes had occurred in the appearance of the surrounding country since the days when Mormon and Moroni had trod the spot where we stood. Still we could readily understand, even now, how admirable a position this would be for a general to occupy in watching and directing the movements of armies and in scrutinizing the position of an enemy.

Around Cumorah is yet a land of many waters, rivers and fountains as Mormon said it was in his day. Our emotions on treading on this sacred hill were of the most peculiar character. They were indescribable. This was the hill Ramah of the Jaredites. In this vicinity, Coriantumr and Shiz, with the people whom they led, fought their last battle. . . . From the summit of this hill, Mormon and his great son Moroni had also witnessed the gathering of hosts of the Nephites, and the . . . myriad legions of their deadly enemies, the Lamanites. Around this hill they had marshaled their forces—their twenty-three divisions of ten thousand men each . . . all to be swept away except Moroni.

It was on this spot that about fourteen hundred years after these events, Joseph Smith, the Prophet, was led by Moroni in person, and here the records, engraved on plates, were committed to him for translation. Who could tread this ground and reflect upon these mighty events, and not be filled with indescribable emotion?[5]

Tragically, a great many of the Nephite records were destroyed by the Lamanites. Even so, enough of the records survived the burning frenzy of the Lamanites to fill a small cave according to Brigham Young, who said on one occasion:

Joseph Smith did not translate all the plates; there was a portion of them sealed, which you can learn from the Book of Doctrine and Covenants. When Joseph got the plates, the angel instructed him to carry them back to the hill Cumorah, which he did. Oliver says that when Joseph and Oliver went there, the hill opened, and they walked into a cave, in which there was a large and spacious room. He says he did not think at the time whether they had the light of the sun or artificial light; but that it was just as light as day. They laid the plates on a table; it was a large table that stood in the room. Under this table there was a pile of plates as much as two feet high, and there were altogether in this room more plates than probably many wagon loads; they were piled up in the corners and along the walls. The first time they went there the sword of Laban hung on the wall; but when they went again it had been taken down and laid upon the table across the gold plates; it was unsheathed, and on it was written these words: "This sword will never be sheathed again until the kingdoms of this world become the kingdom of our God and his Christ."[6]

Joseph F. Smith was firm in his conviction that New York's Hill Cumorah was the same hill mentioned in the scriptures and made every effort make his position known. He said:

From all the evidence in the Book of Mormon, augmented by the testimony of the Prophet Joseph Smith, these final battles took place in the territory known as the United States and in the neighborhood of the Great Lakes and hills of Western New York. And here Moroni found the resting place for the sacred instruments that were committed to his care.[7]

In commenting further on the subject in the *Doctrines of Salvation*, Joseph Fielding Smith said:

It is known that the Hill Cumorah where the Nephites were destroyed is the hill where the Jaredites were also destroyed. This hill was known to the Jaredites as Ramah. It was approximately near to the waters of Ripliancum, which the Book of Ether says, "by interpretation, is large, or to exceed all." Mormon adds: "And it came to pass that we did march forth to the land of Cumorah . . . and it was in a land of many waters, rivers, and fountains; and here we had hope to gain advantage over the Lamanites" [Mormon 6:2–4] . . .

It must be conceded that this description fits perfectly the land of Cumorah in New York. . . . Moreover, the Prophet Joseph Smith himself is on record, definitely declaring the present hill called Cumorah to be the exact hill spoken of in the Book of Mormon.[8]

Joseph Smith's attempt to explain his mission in bringing forth an ancient record of the inhabitants of this country was written, in part, in the Wentworth letter. In referring to the angel Moroni's instructions to him and his recital about the aborigines of America, he said: "I was also informed concerning the aboriginal inhabitants of this country . . . I was also told where were deposited some plates on which were engraven an abridgment of the records of the ancient Prophets that had existed on this continent."[9]

Our own blessed America is the land spoken of by the ancient prophets, and the "Stick of Joseph" deals exclusively with the events that transpired in America—more especially amid the hills and valleys of western New York. While the Nephites spread out into a number of other regions, the story of the Nephite's long sojourn in the promised land began in this region, and after nine centuries of intrigue and warfare, it ended in this region. During that long span of time, righteous men recorded the history of their day and age to preserve a legacy of prophecy and religious insights worthy of our attention and instruction, and to impart that only those who worship God will prosper in the promised land.

Once the Nephites and Hopewell were destroyed, North

American trade dwindled. As more and more time passed, the memory of America soon faded and became lost to history,[10] with geographers thereafter believing that a voyage west from Spain would lead to India and China—the very fact that drove Columbus westward.

Part Nine

After Cumorah

~ **26** ~

Further Cleansing

The cleansing of the promised land in preparation for the rise of the Gentile nation and the latter-day Restoration did not end with the destruction of the Hopewell and the forced migration of the remaining Nahuas/Toltecs into Mexico. Nor did it end with the destruction of the Nephites. The wilder Chichimec tribes still ruled the land in concert with the Lamanites. Their ultimate expulsion from the promised land came five centuries later when the Chichimecs also moved en-mass into Mexico, although voluntarily this time.

The Chichimecs enjoyed a close communication with the Toltecs in Mexico, because Chichimec blood ran through their nobility. It seems that once the Toltecs reached their destination, they called for a monarch. One of the chiefs was chosen to occupy the new throne, but their prophet counseled against it, reminding them that not only had the Chichimecs (wild tribes) been pursuing them, but other enemies—the people they deposed when they entered Mexico and took possession of their lands—were gaining on them as well.

The name Chichimeca was the name that the Nahua people generally applied to the wild tribes in the area, a name similar to the European term *barbarian*, a term that no doubt included the Lamanites, who merged with the Chichimecs once they both began to inhabit the same regions. Seeing how close various Chichimec settlements were to Tollan and fearing the Chichimecs would one day rise up against them and take away their land—especially since their prophet Hueymatzin had already foreseen such a time—the prophet devised a plan to ask for a son of the Chichimecs to act as their king. Such a thing would only be on the condition that they would remain a free people, however, "owing no allegiance whatever to the Chichimecs, although the two powers would enter into an alliance for mutual defense and assistance."[1]

The advice of the venerated old counselor was accepted. Gifts of great value were immediately dispatched back to Huehue Tlapalan, the home of the Chichimecs, where the second son of the king was chosen. He accompanied them back to Tollan and crowned their king. To safeguard their futures, the Nahuas married him to a Toltec lady of high birth, and at the time of his coronation they set a rule in place that no one would rule more than fifty-two years. All the rights of the coronation were held in Teotihuacan, for although Tollan was the capital, Nahua records imply that the "supremacy attributed to the priesthood of Tollan . . . was really exercised by the priests of the sun at Teotihuacan."[2] Surprisingly, the young Chichimec chosen as king was so amiable and intelligent that the Toltecs revered him, so much so, that all the Nahua nations in the region gave their allegiance to this new monarch. He ruled Tollan for the full fifty-two years.

The worship of their combined forces included the same rituals practiced in the mound-building regions of the Mississippi and Ohio valleys. Although a supreme being was venerated above all, in time their worship included the worship of the other gods, such as the sun and the moon gods, whose images they honored in elaborately decorated temples. The sun-god in both lands was considered the god of sustenance. His wife represented the moon. They also had other gods representing brothers and sisters of the sun and moon, along with other idols that they worshipped clear up to the time of the Spanish invasion.

According to Ixtlilxochitl, although the Toltecs ultimately became an idolatrous people, they did not sacrifice men and did not follow the superstitious sacrifices imposed upon the empire by the later Aztecs, except to their god, Tlaloc, to whom they sacrificed certain maidens and the greatest evil-doers in the land at certain times of the year. While various rulers sanctioned human sacrifice, due to their early kings having Chichimec blood, others vehemently opposed it and did everything they could to abolish it from their lands. At certain times and under certain rulers, the Lord sent plagues upon the land to reinforce his displeasure with their lust for human flesh, while at other times he blessed and prospered those who honored his ways.

So the saga went from generation to generation, until five centuries had passed, with both good and bad monarchs ruling the land. Then, in the tenth century, a ruler was placed on the throne that brought about the nation's destruction—Topiltzin Quetzalcoatl.

Although Quetzalcoatl is the name of one of the gods of the Nahuatl race, that name-title was also bestowed upon their ruling high priest as well, and many of their kings. In spite of the name's common use, the singular name "Quetzalcoatl" is almost always associated with King Topiltzin, who ruled the Toltec empire in the tenth century. To avoid confusion, I will refer to him by the joint name, Topiltzin Quetzalcoatl, rather than Quetzalcoatl.

The rule of king Topiltzin Quetzalcoatl brought the Toltec

empire to its greatest cultural level, and its influence was felt over a large part of Mexico for the next four hundred years, long after the fall of Tollan. Although Topiltzin Quetzalcoatl began his reign as a righteous king, in time he succumbed to temptations, plunged into lasciviousness and riotous living, and brought about the fulfillment of various prophecies that predicted the doom of the empire. Vice had taken complete possession of the empire and had even spread to cities and provinces not under the immediate authority of Tollan. The unscrupulous began to rule, crimes went unpunished, and the government was in chaos, much as things had been back in Zarahemla before the end came

for the Nephites. Through prayer and sacrifice, the priests tried to appease the gods, but the vice flowing across the land went completely unchecked. The fate of the kingdom was sealed, and the Toltecs never knew peace again. The successive plagues that hit the region killed thousands of Toltecs, and more deaths followed as warfare with neighboring regions began.

It was the cunning and might of rival factions that finally toppled King Topiltzin from his throne, where we now find him hiding away in a swamp until it was safe to emerge. He then secretly traveled to a rich province somewhere along the South Sea (the Gulf of Mexico—likely Florida) and told some followers his intentions of returning to Huehue Tlapalan. He promised that once he arrived, he would ask the Chichimec Emperor to intercede in their behalf knowing he alone had the power to crush his enemies.

The demoralized and dethroned king Topiltzin apparently felt his last hope of destroying his enemies lay with those whose own royal blood flowed through the ruling class of Tollan. We might remember that when the Toltec exiles from Huehue Tlapalan first entered Mexico, they entreated the Chichimec emperor to provide a king so the two nations might live in peace. Thus, the Toltec Empire was ruled by two bloodlines, the Chichimec and the Toltec. The wife of the young Chichimec king was of Toltec blood, as were most of his subjects. After committing his two infant children to a faithful guardian to be raised ignorant of their royal birth, Topiltzin Quetzalcoatl left the country, promising his followers that one day he would "return to punish his foes."[3] Shortly thereafter he and a number of Toltec companions departed through the wilderness for Tlapalan.

Ixtlilxochitl reports that Topiltzin reached Huehue Tlapalan in safety and was actually greeted warmly by the Chichimec emperor who had just recently succeeded to the throne. Hoping to avenge his people, "Topiltzin gave all his rights to the kingdom of Tollan" to this new Chichimec emperor "on condition that he would punish [his] enemies." The emperor agreed.[4]

As the story continues, the son of the Chichimec emperor, Xolotl, instructed all his nobles to be ready to accompany him to Tollan within the space of six months. Ixtlilxochitl and Veytia both claim that "no less than three million two hundred and two thousand men and women, besides children rallied to his standard, leaving one million six hundred thousand subjects of Acuahtzin, and thus making it not a mere expedition but a decided emigration."[5]

Upon arriving in Mexico, the Chichimecs found the streets deserted and overgrown with vegetation and its magnificent temples and palaces in ruins. Only desolation remained where there had once been a mighty metropolis that Ixtlilxochitl claims collapsed in AD 959.

Of the Toltecs who survived the terrible wars and plagues that caused the destruction of the mighty Tollan, some stayed, but others preferred to travel to the lands farther south that had suffered less destruction than those in the north. Some took refuge in the Miztec and Zapotec provinces of Oajaca, while others crossed into Guatemala and Yucatan, where they became especially influential in molding the future political events among the Maya. Early writers say that others founded settlements on the coasts

of both oceans, from which parties ultimately returned at subsequent periods and reestablish themselves in Mexico. Others crossed the Isthmus of Tehuantepec and passed into South America, and others set sail into the Pacific Ocean in search of new homes.

It is commonly believed that the dethroned Topiltzin headed one of the colonies in the Yucatan Peninsula, where he hoped to build up another wealthy empire now that Tollan was lost. Actually, the Maya, who began to blossom in Yucatan around 200 BC, flourished as one of the regions grandest civilizations for several centuries, but sometime between the seventh and ninth centuries fell into decay. The arrival of Topiltzin and his followers rejuvenated the dying Maya civilization by introducing the Maya to Toltec religion, Toltec architecture, and Toltec art. So much artwork has been found in Central America that most scholars readily recognize Toltec influence among the Maya during various periods in history, and they suggest that it was they who subsequently built many of the magnificent cities found scattered throughout the region.

As to Topiltzin, the Popol Vuh adds he ultimately returned to Huehue Tlapalan, traveling over the deserts by night. He arrived at the place he lived for another thirty years, served and showered with gifts by the people of Tlapalan and dying at the age of 104.[6]

27

The Mississippi Culture

A fter the fall of the Toltec Empire, some of the empire's subjects filtered back into the lands of their ancient mound-
building fathers, starting a new mound-building era along the
Mississippi River that had striking similarities to their cousin's
cultures in Mexico. When John McIntosh asked the Natchez (a
southern branch of the
Mississippi culture)
about their ancestry,
they responded that
their most ancient
fathers had come
from the direction
of the rising sun, but
after a long journey
that almost caused
their extinction (the
forced migration of

*A mound village in Illinois
by Herbert Rowe*

the Toltecs from Huehue Tlapalan), they said they came to live yonder, pointing to the southwest toward Mexico. There they claim to have maintained themselves for a long time, but when enemy forces invaded and sent many of their people to the hills, their Great Sun sent some of the people up the Mississippi to explore the region and see if it was fit for habitation. In time, they returned with such good news about the bounties of the lands to the east of the great river that he ordered all his subjects on the plains to move to this new location and there to "build a temple, and to preserve the *eternal fire.*"[1]

The heartland of this new culture was mainly in the central Mississippi Valley in Cahokia, Illinois, where it flourished between AD 800 and AD 1500. Various satellite sites spanned half the continent from Wisconsin all the way to the Gulf of Mexico, from Georgia to Tennessee, Ohio, Illinois, and Arkansas, and from Texas to Oklahoma.

Interestingly, the great mound at Cahokia, Illinois, is bigger than the pyramid at Teotihuacan whose sides measure 752 feet in length. The pyramid at Cahokia measures 1,003 feet in length, making it the largest pyramid in the world. Whether it was a temple mound is still a matter of debate; however, it is generally accepted that the flat level summit of this and other such pyramids was the place their chiefs, or Great Suns, resided. Unfortunately, with the rise of Cahokia, sun-worship slipped right back into the promised land, with

Monk's Mound at Cahokia

their worship now expanded to include fire which burned perpetually throughout the year on top of their pyramid-type structures. As time passed, the fire became a part of the worship of their Fire God—the Sun.

From Conant we read:

> Upon these [pyramids] burned the perpetual fires, to be extinguished only at the close of the years, and rekindled by the sun himself, as his rising beams were consecrated by the high priests, when the new year began. This event was always observed with the greatest solemnity.
>
> When the sacred flame expired upon the altars, with the dying year, the whole land was filled with gloom, and the fire upon every domestic hearth must be extinguished also. Then the people sat down in awful suspense to watch for the morning. Possibly their father, the sun, might be angry with his children, and veil his glory behind the clouds and the coming dawn. Then as they thought of their sins and bewailed their transgressions, their fears were expressed in loud lamentations. But as the expected dawn—the momentous time— approaches, all eyes are turned towards the holy mount where the now fireless altar stands. At length the eastern sky begins to glow with a golden light which tells them that their god is near, and, while they watch, he rolls in splendor from behind the eastern hills, and darts his fiery beams upon the sacred place where holy men are waiting to ignite anew the sacrificial fires. Nor do they wait in vain, for soon the curling smoke and the signal flames are seen by the breathless multitude which fill the plains below, and then one long, glad shout is heard and songs of joy salute the bright new year. Swift-footed messengers receive the new-lit fire from the hands of the priests, quickly it is distributed to the waiting throng and carried exultingly to their several homes, when all begin the joyful celebration of the feast of the sun.[2]

No one knows why the culture ultimately collapsed and its cities were abandoned. But whatever the reason, it is believed that some of their astronomer-priests resettled in southern Wisconsin. Here, Carl Muck claims they re-created a similar settlement three miles east of Rock Lake, a place some reconcile with one of the stopping places of the proto-Aztecs (one of the seven sub-tribes of the Nahuas) before their southward migration into Mexico. Their route appears to have taken them through the four corners area of Arizona, Utah, Colorado, and New Mexico. During a sermon in the old Tabernacle in Salt Lake City, Brigham Young stated: "There are scores of evil spirits here—spirits of the old Gadianton Robbers. . . . There are millions of those spirits in the mountains."[3]

Whatever route the proto-Aztecs took into Mexico was ultimately forgotten in time. The Aztecs believe their god created the great desert, which now separates the United States from Mexico so that they would remain in the south and fulfill their destinies in that part of the world. But it is more likely that it was the god of Israel who caused the land to dry up in his efforts to keep the Aztecs from returning to the promised land, because they were a decadent and wicked people.

It is said the Aztecs arrived in Mexico sometime in the twelfth century, and they built the beautiful city of Tenochtitlan soon after, a city on an island in Mexico that became a stronghold for the Aztecs for years to come. According to Aztec legends, their god, Huitzilopochtli, had directed them to found a city on the site where they would see an eagle devouring a snake perched on a fruit-bearing nopal cactus. We might remember that the symbol of Dan was a serpent. Yet Dan also appears to be associated with the eagle. The emblem of the tribe of Dan was the serpent in fulfillment of Jacob's prophecy in Genesis 49:17: "Dan shall be a serpent by the way, an adder in the path, that biteth the horse heels, so that his rider shall fall backward." However, from Unger's *Bible Dictionary* we read: "To Dan was given the symbol of Scorpio, which, in the ancient Egyptian zodiac was a snake. However, when the time came to hoist the symbol of the snake, Ahiezer refused, and chose instead the symbol of an eagle. . . . 'The standard of the tribe was of white and red, and the crest upon it, an eagle, the great foe to serpents, which had been chosen by the leader instead of a serpent, because Jacob

Coat of Arms for Mexico

had compared Dan to a serpent.'"[4] An eagle and a serpent is now depicted on the coat of arms of Mexico.

As grand as their cities were, the reign of the Aztecs was one of horror. Their worship led to the practice of human sacrifice and ritual cannibalism on an unprecedented scale. The Maya and Nahua both nourished the gods by drawing their own blood. They pierced their tongues, ears, extremities, or genitals. But the Aztecs took bloodletting to new heights by adopting the belief that human hearts were the most nourishing of all and the braver the victim the more nourishing the sacrifice. This false notion led to the widespread wars that followed this unholy people, all for the purpose of capturing sacrificial victims. We learn from Aztec history that Ahuitzotl (1468–1502), who preceded Moctezuma II as king, sacrificed twenty thousand people after one campaign alone.

These were a wicked and perverse people who enjoyed dressing in the flayed skins of their sacrificial victims. In reaction to such depravity, the people once again began to favor the rival deities and priesthood, and looked to the Plumed (feathered) Serpent for relief from their woes. Their prayers were unexpectedly answered when Spanish invaders made their appearance along their eastern shores. Thinking Cortez was a god, the oppressed natives welcomed him with open arms and were more than ready to embrace the new faith offered them by their conquerors.

⟁ 28 ⟁

Lamanite Migrations

It was now safe for many of the more righteous Lamanites to come home, for over the course of centuries some were led away from the wicked sun-worshipping centers in the north-east. Jacob, the brother of Nephi, mentions this in an address to his people.

> O all ye that are pure in heart, lift up your heads and receive the pleasing word of God, and feast upon his love; for ye may, if your minds are firm, forever.
>
> But, wo, wo, unto you that are not pure in heart, that are filthy this day before God; for except ye repent the land is cursed for your sakes; and the Lamanites, which are not filthy like unto you, nevertheless they are cursed with a sore cursing, shall scourge you even unto destruction.
>
> And the time speedily cometh, that except ye repent they shall possess the land of your inheritance, and the Lord God will lead away the righteous out from among you.
>
> Behold, the Lamanites your brethren, whom ye hate because of their filthiness and the cursing which hath come upon their skins, are more righteous than you; for they have

not forgotten the commandment of the Lord, which was given unto our father. (Jacob 3:1–5)

The "Red Record" of the Lenni Lenape tribes, also called the *Walam Olum*, maintains that the Lenni Lenape once lived in a region far to the northwest. Heckewelder claims their ancestors came from of a land of ice and snow in the far northwest of this continent.[1] In 1951, Milton R. Hunter reported to the Church committee on Indian Relations and to the President of the Quorum of the Twelve Apostles that the Iroquois told him: "The historical Indians we call 'Delaware' which anciently were known as the Lenni Lenapees, did indeed come from the west in great numbers. That in times past they desired to return to their original homeland in the east along the Atlantic seaboard."[2]

It appears that a branch of the Lamanites left the northeast early in their history, only to return ninety-six generations later to the lands of their fathers. Their trek home is said to have included crossing a great chasm of water that had frozen over, allowing them to cross to the other side in just one night. Once across, they headed south. David McCrutchen suggests the two Algonquin-speaking tribes in California, the Yuroks and Wiyot, may have originated from the Lenape who remained behind after the main body crossed the Rockies on their journey east. There in the shadows of what appear to be the great Rocky Mountains, a young chief had a vision about the lands to the east of the Appalachian Mountains. Upon hearing of it, the head priests and the elders fasted in hopes of receiving further light and knowledge on the subject—a practice consistent with Israelite

traditions. After three days of fasting, the Great Spirit spoke to them and gently urged them to make the journey. They packed the bones of their ancestors onto dog-sleds, along with provisions for the journey, and made ready to go.[3]

Once on the plains, they were faced with warfare from the indigenous people of the region. To make matters worse, they claim to have endured a civil war of their own. Only after many years of warfare did they chose to continue their journey east to the place their fathers saw in vision. Their journey eastward was not uninterrupted, however, for along the way they encountered still another tribe of strangers. Fearlessly, they approached these strangers with a black wampum belt in one hand (a declaration of war) and a peace pipe in the other and asked them which they preferred. The strangers, now thought to be a colony of Iroquois who appear to have lived further west at this time, chose the peace pipe, and the two became friends and allies and promised to assist each other if the need ever arose.

That need arose when the Lenape encounter the Allegheny Indians, or the Talligewi (the old name for the Cherokee) living in great cities east of the Mississippi River. While the Telgas gave permission for the Lenni Lenape to cross the river and settle lands further east, once they saw their immense numbers, they changed their minds and attacked, massacring all those who had already crossed over. Angry by such treachery, the Lenape retaliated, and a war commenced that lasted for many years. In fact, four sachems lived out their terms as sovereigns before the Lenape and their Iroquois allies finally succeeded in their attempts to claim the land, at which time the Cherokee fled down the Mississippi River and were never heard from again.[4] The gentler Lenape took over the fertile valley abandoned by the Allegewi (Cherokee), and the Iroquois were given the lands to the north around the Great Lakes—their old ancestral stomping grounds.

The government of the Lenape tribes stressed freedom and equality among their tribes. Perhaps the Lenape were among those the Lord led out of the territory from time to time to protect them from the pollution of the Hopewell and other sun-worshiping tribes until they had been destroyed.

Ultimately, the Lenape continued their long migration east until they reached the lush green country along the Delaware River that led to the Great Eastern Sea. Here they stood at the edge of the world, the home of their dreams, which the Red Record claims they reached in AD 1396. Three of their greatest chiefs bore the name Tamanend, all warmly remembered as paragons of ancient virtue, warmth, bravery, generosity, and openheartedness. The third was the chief who met William Penn for the Great Treaty of 1682 once the times of the Gentiles commenced.

The Algonquin Migration

The Algonquins also endured a long migration, but it was a little closer to home. According to Grandfather William Commanda, keeper of the Seven Fires Wampum Belt of the Algonquin people, somewhere in a period before AD 1000–1400, a vision was shown those living along the shores of the Great Salt Water, which some take to be the Atlantic Ocean near the Saint Lawrence River. They were told that if more of the Ojibway did not move further west, they would not be able to keep their traditional ways alive, because a new people were destined to arrive and would change their lifestyle forever. After receiving assurance from their *allied brothers*, the Micmac, and *father* Abenaki that it was okay to pass through their territory, they proceeded to advance along the river to the first of seven stopping places and their prophesied destination, each of which would be distinguishable by a shining migis (cowry) shell.

Grandfather Commanda claimed that ten thousand canoes filled with people were soon seen heading toward the Great Lakes in a migration that some say took 500 years. They separated at seven places they found the migis shell: 1) Montreal, Quebec, where they stayed a long time. Then, while others continued their journey up the Saint Lawrence River, one group detoured into the Ottawa

An Ojibway chief
"One called from a distance"

River, where they would come to be known as the Algonkin; 2) Niagara Falls; 3) the Detroit River; 4) Manitoulin Island in Lake Huron; 5) Sault St. Marie in Lake Superior; 6) Spirit Island in Duluth Michigan; and 7) Madeline Island in the Apostle Islands of Lake Superior. All were places once occupied by their ancient fathers, and a little more secure than New England, which was destined to receive an influx of Gentiles in the near future.

Part Ten

The Times of the Gentiles

—❧ **29** ❧—

The Times of the Gentiles

I t appears the promised land did not incorporate the entire hemi-sphere, just the territory contained in what today is the United States of America—a land destined to become the greatest, most powerful nation on earth. Christopher Columbus's voyage to the Bahamas in 1492 initiated the age of exploration and led to the discovery of the New World, although he himself never set foot on the promised land itself, nor opened it up to European trade. Columbus landed near Central America in 1502, five years after John Cabot discovered North America and Amerigo Vespucci discovered South America, with the lat-ter's name given the entire hemispheric mainland.

Several names crop up when search-ing for the true discoverer of America. One of the first is an Irish monk named

Christopher Columbus

The voyage of
St. Brendan, the monk

St. Brendan, one of the twelve apostles of Ireland. It is said to he arrived in North America in AD 545, after setting sail from Ireland in search of a mysterious island called the "Promised Land of the Saints." The descriptions he gives of the places and landmarks he saw along the way lead many to believe he was in Maine or Nova Scotia, which earned him the title of the first to discover America.

Another name often considered is Leif Eriksson. The *Sagas of Iceland* tells us that after converting to Christianity, he set sail from Greenland to explore the lands to the west in AD 1002. Three lands were discovered: Helluland, which some take to be Baffin Island; Markland, believed to be Labrador; and Vineland, meaning the land of wine, thought be either Labrador or Massachusetts, where a small colony was planted. However, the British continue to insist it was St. Brandon who first arrived in America. Moreover, they believe his name is worthy of being reintroduced into the pages of history as the true discoverer of America, or the "Promised Land of the Saints," as he called it. Actually that was a pretty fitting name for America, because a number of Israelites had been transplanted in America long before Columbus, not just the Nephites and Mulekites. St. Brendan may have

Leif Eriksson's voyage westward

had prior knowledge of several Irish Danites. Some believe Columbus was looking for St. Brendan's Isle when he discovered the West Indies. On the eve of his great voyage in 1492, he wrote: "I am convinced that the terrestrial paradise is the Island of St. Brendan, which none can reach save by the will of God."

It was apparently not the will of God that Columbus set foot on the promised land of St. Brendan, because his mind was set upon riches while St. Brendan's was a mission to the faithful followers of Christ. Even so, while Columbus is not regarded to be the first to discover what came to be called America, it was his adventures that began a series of explorations which resulted in the ultimate discovery and colonization of North America. However, because nearly five centuries separated the voyages of St. Brendan and Leif Eriksson, with another five centuries passing before further exploration began, it is now becoming widely accepted that the first European to reach North America was John Cabot who claimed North America for the crown of England in 1497.

Cabot's descriptions suggests he landed somewhere along the east coast of America between Maine and Labrador and then sailed south along the east coast before returning home—claiming it all for England. His voyage set the stage for further exploration and the ultimate colonization of North America, and thus he was likely the man noted in 1 Nephi 13:12.

> And I looked and beheld a man among the Gentiles, who was separated from the seed of my brethren by the many waters; and I beheld the Spirit of God, that it came down and wrought upon the man; and he went forth upon the many waters, even unto the seed of my brethren, who were in the promised land.

There is no reason to suppose that Columbus was the only man moved upon by the Holy Spirit to explore the lands to the west. Many of our early explorers were Christians, including

John Cabot

Cabot, who was a member of the religious fraternity of St. John. Being the first to land on American soil since Leif Eriksson, Cabot opened up the Grand Banks off Newfoundland to a steady stream of European fishermen, For the next century, one thousand European fishing fleets used the Grand banks for cod. The success they enjoyed set the stage for the eventual colonization of North America, with Cabot's adventures serving as a foundation for England's later claims to the continent.

The scripture 1 Nephi 13:13 makes it clear that many were moved upon by the Holy Ghost to explore the lands to the west. "And it came to pass that I beheld the Spirit of God, that it wrought upon other Gentiles; and they went forth out of captivity, upon the many waters." True to the scriptures, many more followed, including Giovanni da Verrazano. His encounter with the Micmac branch of the Algonquins in Maine led to rumors of a rich and powerful native kingdom and more people came to the area.

Samuel de Champlain soon followed and founded Quebec for the French. Henry Hudson, another English sea captain, believed he could find a northwest passage to Asia. After exploring the east coast of America, he informed the Netherlands that the mainland was rich in natural resources, which brought still more Gentiles into the area, this time from Holland.

Jesuit priests also arrived from

the Old World. However, they were much more interested in converting the Indians than feeding them, because the French Catholic Church wanted to establish a utopian Christian community in the colony. Little did they know that the Savior himself had once walked these lands and that these were his people, remnants of the house of Israel from the tribe of Joseph, and that this was

Verrazano's voyage west

their promised land, a land the Lord would not take from them, notwithstanding the upcoming trials they were about to endure.

With news of the New World quickly spreading across Europe, Christians of all faiths sailed to America in search of religious freedom. In 1602, the Mayflower set sail with 102 pilgrims from Plymouth, England, to America, where they founded Plymouth, Massachusetts. Once on American soil their dreams of a better life were finally realized, because they could now live their religion in peace. A day of thanksgiving was set and they shared a feast with the Indians. Other Gentiles soon followed. They initially came in small groups, then in shiploads, all looking to escape persecution of one kind or another and to have the liberty and freedom to worship as they pleased. Although they were of many faiths, they all worshiped Jesus Christ.

Several nations vied for control of America's vast natural resources. France had

Jesuit Priests among the natives

succeeded in acquiring a large territory in the middle of the country; England was holding territory along the east coast, and Spain, which now held much of the West Indies and Mexico, looked wantonly at the lands to the north. War eventually broke out, and it raged back and forth for the next seven years, until the French were finally defeated and turned over their heartland to the English in 1763, keeping only Canada for themselves.

Twelve years after the British defeated the French, the American Revolutionary War broke out. George Washington played a pivotal role in that war, which after much prayer to the God of the land, went in favor of the colonists. The new gentile colonists were delivered out of the hands of all the other nations, just as described in 1 Nephi 13:16–19.

> And it came to pass that I, Nephi, beheld that the Gentiles . . . had gone forth out of captivity. . . . And I beheld that their mother Gentiles were gathered together upon the waters . . . to battle against them. . . . And I, Nephi, beheld that the Gentiles that had gone out of captivity were delivered by the power of God out of the hands of all other nations (1 Nephi 13:16–19).

The Indians fought with the Gentiles over territorial rights, some on one side, and some on the other, with some simply fighting among themselves. The end of the Revolutionary War finally brought peace to the land, but not to the American Indians. The white settlers still feared their wild ways. Many were placed in reservations, and others were sent on forced migrations to unsettled lands to the west of the Mississippi River.

Treaties were made with the Indians as early as 1817. The Cherokee agreed to move to the west of the Mississippi in eastern Kansas bordering Missouri, which was the fringe of the newly formed United States, where they would now be known as the county's western tribes of Indians. While some moved voluntarily,

Trail of Tears

others resisted. Thus, President Andrew Jackson set things in motion to force them west, and thousands died on the way on this "Trail of Tears."

The New England Lenni Lenape, those honored as "Grandfathers," were taken to portions of eastern Oklahoma. The Iroquois were also moved, but because of fraudulent dealings, they were able to retain their reservations. This relates to a large part of Lehi's children settling far from the lands of their fathers. Yet the Lord knew where they were. In a revelation given through the Prophet Joseph Smith to Newell Knight in Doctrine and Covenants 54:8, the Lord instructed Newell to flee his enemies and go west to Missouri—to the borders of the Lamanites, right where so many of the displaced seed of Lehi were living.

30

Hiawatha

John McIntosh described the Iroquois as a poor and barbarous people who were bred under the darkest ignorance yet exhibited a noble genius, and that no Roman hero had a greater love for country and a contempt for death than the Iroquois. Although a fierce and barbarous race, they are at the same time "polite and manage all their affairs judiciously. Because of their self perceived superiority, they call themselves, Ongu-honwe, meaning, 'men surpassing all others.'" Unfortunately, their long confinement in the mountains left them ignorant of spiritual matters. They were in need of instruction—instruction not tainted by the dark philosophies of those around them.

That instruction came when a teacher arrived among them and taught the Iroquois a peace religion. He came in the name of the greatest of all spirits and told the people that it was the Father's will that his kingdom should be established upon this land, but that the people must live his laws first. He taught them the two great laws: "Love Manito (the Lord) above all else, and love each other as you wish to be loved." He predicted that a messenger would come later in time and give them more instructions.

More changes took place in the sixteenth century. With the Restoration of the gospel only a few centuries away, more work had to be done to prepare the promised land for the rise of the new Gentile nation, a nation founded on the principles of equality and justice so the Restoration could take place. Through inspiration, the Lord raised up Hiawatha, a great orator instrumental in setting the stage for this nation's rise to power as a land of liberty among the Gentiles. Hiawatha presented the idea of a unique league of nations. He first presented it to his own people in New York sometime around the middle of the sixteenth century in the region of the Finger Lakes, not too far from the Hill Cumorah.

Three main figures show up in the story of the formation of the Iroquois's League of Nations. The first, named Atotarho, practiced the dark arts and destroyed families by way of secret murders, which suggests his ties to the Gadianton Robbers. He was described as a wizard and a fierce man so hated that he was depicted in artwork as having hair made of writhing snakes—a not-so-pretty picture, but one apparently fitting. He was described as haughty, stern, crafty, and a remorseless tyrant. It was said he could kill people even at a distance from where he was by virtue of his magic arts. Not surprisingly, no one wanted to cross him, because he tolerated nobody and killed those who attempted to rise above him.

The second leading figure in the founding of the Iroquois League was Hiawatha, an Onondaga chief of high rank, past middle age but greatly loved by his people because of his benevolent nature and wisdom. Unfortunately he was consumed in grief because many of his friends and family members, including all his daughters, had been killed by the wicked sorcerer Atotarho, although he had been spared. He was also feeling the pains of his people who were suffering untold misery because of the never-ending wars that were tearing apart his nation. Hence, he spent a considerable amount of time in contemplation and in devising an elaborate scheme for a vast confederacy that would ensure his people's lasting peace. Most of the tribes had already been involved in one type of confederacy or another. The one he envisioned would not be a loose transitory league, but a permanent government, with the hope it would involve all the tribes and abolish war altogether.

After working out the particulars in his own mind, Hiawatha presented the plan to his own people in a grand council meeting. Unfortunately, Atotarho was there, and his fearsome appearance and scowl of disapproval totally overwhelmed the congregation, and they backed away from the proposal. A second counsel produced the same results. When a third attempt failed to bring even one person to the meeting, Hiawatha left disheartened, and he sat down on the ground with his buried his head in the folds of his mantle and remained there a long time bowed down in grief and sorrow. Once composing himself, he arose and headed out of town toward the southeast.

At length, Hiawatha came to a Mohawk town where he hoped to converse with chief Dekanawidah, an Onondaga by birth, but adopted by the Mohawk. Dekanawidah is the third person in the formation of the Iroquois League of Nations. It is said he arrived in the land after crossing Lake Ontario in a white canoe, a most holy man known for his powerful vision—most likely a prophet with prophetic insights. Hiawatha felt that if he could entice Dekanawidah to at least hear about the confederacy, he might help the league come to fruition.

Once the two chiefs met, Dekanawidah liked Hiawatha's plan immediately, and after perfecting it between themselves, presented it to the Mohawk, who also accepted it readily, because

The Tree of Peace

the plan enunciated principles of justice and equality and that bloodshed must yield to a new sense of brotherhood. This new Law of Peace laid out a government of the people, by the people, and for the people, with three branches, each of which amounted to a faith based on reason and thinking. The prophet then described a great Tree of Peace under whose branches the tribes would meet to resolve their differences.

Dekanawidah then sent for a representative from the Oneida, who also accepted it. Then the time came to present it once again to the Oneida (or rather to Atotarho) for approval, but he coldly rejected it, just as he had before. They went to the Cayugas, the most genial of the Iroquois tribes, who needed little persuasion and who joined the Mohawk and Oneida representatives in a new embassy to the Onondagas, with the Onondagas chosen as the leading nation in the league.

Dekanawidah and Hiawatha then traveled the length and breadth of Iroquois country, forging alliances and teaching the laws of justice. One by one, each village and town was converted to this new change in government and eventually met at Onondaga Lake in New York for a grand council of the newly united nations.

The first meeting was held by fifty chiefs under a giant evergreen tree. An eagle was perched in it scanning the horizon for any signs of trouble. They were taught that the great law of peace provided for a society governed by liberty, dignity, and harmony. Then Dekanawidah was said to have uprooted a white pine, exposing a deep cavern with a river at its bottom. He instructed his warriors to cast their weapons into this hole and then watched as the river carried them into the bowels of the earth. Replanting the tree, the prophet said: "This burying the hatchet is the end of killing and war."

The vision of Hiawatha of a united confederacy, which was put into practice by Dekanawidah, ultimately put an end to much of the incessant feuding between the tribes, although not all. But the combined strength of the league gave the Iroquois a dominance that continued to shape the region's history for years to come. In fact, the Founding Fathers of the United States found their best working model for their new government was not in the writings of European nations, but with the Iroquois League; the great Law of Peace provided both model and incentive to transform thirteen separate colonies into the United States. The Tree of Peace ultimately

The Founding Fathers sign the Declaration of Independence

became the Tree of Liberty, and the eagle, clutching a bundle of thirteen arrows, became the symbol of the new American government. Thus, the Iroquois were instrumental in the formation of the United States government, a government created for the benefit of both the American Indians and the Gentiles, but of particular importance in setting the stage for the Restoration of the gospel of Christ as found in the history of the American tribes, the Book of Mormon.

~ 31 ~

The Iroquois Prophet, Handsome Lake

Because of their numbers and skills as warriors, both the Iroquois and the Algonquins were formidable enemies when the settlers arrived. Their large settlements, which ranged from hamlets to villages of several hundred people, were large enough to ward off the settlers' advances despite their superior weapons. But these foreign colonists brought a weapon from which the Iroquois and Algonquins could not hide nor defend themselves—disease and hard liquor.

While alcohol was deadly for the American Indians, in one instance it brought about the reformation of not only a man but his entire nation. The story of Handsome Lake, a Seneca Iroquois of the Turtle Clan, is a story of conversion, repentance, and hope. He was born along New York's Genesee River in 1735, the land said to have been the Iroquois ancestral domain. He was described as being of average stature, beyond his youth, of having a dread disease of some kind, and of being hopelessly addicted to the "firewater." In fact, many of his people were struggling with the same addiction and found themselves unable to manage their everyday affairs, let alone be worried about their futures.

For four years Handsome Lake lay as a hopeless invalid under the care of his married daughter and her husband in a dilapidated old cabin, which barely kept the elements out. His unspecified illness was totally debilitating and made all the worse by his use of alcohol. He knew this but persisted all the same, which added to his guilt and made him feel completely worthless before the Great Spirit. Even so, he thought of him often. As the sunlight poured into his room each morning, he knew that the Creator had provided the light and warmth. When he heard the birds sing, he thanked the Great Ruler for their music. He looked up through the chimney at night and saw the stars and knew the Great Ruler had created them and was thankful. He implored the great Father of the sky-world that he might live, for he had wasted away to nothing more than yellow skin and bones during his four years of confinement and was not sure he could make it through even one more day.

One morning, his daughter, who was just outside the cabin, heard her father cry out. Startled, she looked up to see her father coming toward her, but he was teetering out of control. She immediately rushed to catch him, but he fell dying at her feet. She and her husband carried him inside, dressed him for burial, and sent for their relatives to say their last good-bye. Yet, strangely, those who were mourning him noticed that a part of his body was still warm. They waited for three full days as Handsome Lake remained in a coma. Once awakened, Handsome Lake reported to his family and friends that he had been to upper world where he had met four beings who guided him through a series of visionary experiences. He was then to take these experiences back to the earth-world and teach his people. Handsome Lake said, "Never have I experienced such wondrous visions."

As his recitation of events continued, he explained that only three holy men bid him welcome when he arrived, saying, "He who created the world at the beginning employed us to come to earth. He commanded us saying: Go once more down upon the earth and visit him who thinks of me. He is grateful for my creations, moreover he wishes to rise from sickness and walk upon the earth. Go help him recover."[4] The three messengers then gave Handsome Lake some berries that once prepared for him by his people would make him well.

While the Iroquois still believed in the Great Spirit, they had other deities as well, such as four lessor gods, and the Thunderers who were their grandfathers, and the sun, moon, and the earth, who also bestowed blessings. Even witches and fairies had their place—more Irish influence. The time had come to bring back to a knowledge of the God of their ancient fathers and prepare them for a time in the not too distant future when the glad news of the gospel would be restored.

As Handsome Lake proceeded, he explained that the three messengers led him on the great sky road to the Creator's abode and that "they smelled the fragrant odors of the flowers along the road. Delicious looking fruits were growing on the wayside and every kind of bird flew in the air above them. The most marvelous and beautiful things were on every hand. And all these things were on the heaven road" (Section 112, The Great Message).

More was yet to come, for their journey on the sky road led them to the sky-world itself, where they would meet the fourth messenger. While there they said they would show Handsome Lake the "journey of our friends, and the works of the living of earth. More, you will see the house of the punisher and the lands of our Creator" (Section 82, Code of Handsome Lake).

Just as promised, he was greeted by the spirit of a relative, and even an old pet dog, and saw the fate of the righteous and the wicked who were held captive by the wicked one, which he described as a frightful demon. Yet, as grand as all this was, meeting and conversing with the fourth messenger would be the grandest of all, for it appears the messenger was the Savior himself. After showing him the wounds in his hands and feet and the spear mark in his side, the Savior taught Handsome Lake a variety of laws and commanded him to take them back to his people.

Among myriad other instructions given the prophet, the first and foremost was that the Creator made every living creature, and that he and he alone should be worshipped. Among those things forbidden, four were of particular importance and had to be stopped immediately: 1) Drinking hard liquor; 2) witchcraft, which the Iroquois say was introduced to them by another tribe; 3) the use of charms and amulets; and 4) abortion, with any who indulged in such offenses in need of sore repentance.

Handsome Lake returned to the land of the living and spent the next sixteen years teaching what is referred to as "Gai'wiio," to his countrymen. His prophetic mission impacted his Iroquois brothers, although not without a struggle by certain dissenters, especially Corn Planter, his brother. But in time, the old ways of the Iroquois were done away with and are simply referred to as their Old Testament, and the new, their Long-House religion. From *The Civil, Religious and Mourning Councils and Ceremonies of Adoption of the New York Indians,* we learn the philosophy, or religion, referred to as Gai'wiio, is much like the code of all Christian nations.

Handsome Lake spent the rest of his life imparting this code of law to his countrymen. As his life and mission drew to a close, he came to Tonawanda Reservation by the swamps, which still exist by the borders of old Lake Tonawanda in western New York. He had been invited to preach in Onondaga in central New York. A vision opened up to him that told him that in going he would be singing his "death song," but that he was to go anyway. In seeing the need of their countrymen at Onondaga, the four messengers said: "They have stretched out their hands pleading for you to come, and they are your own people at Onondaga" (Section 122).

Quite a group went with him to Onondaga, which brought Handsome Lake great comfort. Once settled on the borders of Onondaga he told his followers, "I will soon go to my new home. Soon I step into the new world, for there is a plain pathway before me leading there. Whomever follows my teaching will follow in my footsteps and I will look back upon him with outstretched arms inviting him into the new world of our Creator. Alas, I fear that a pass of smoke will obscure the eyes of many from the truth of Gai'wiio, but I pray that when I am gone that all may do what I have taught."[1] He then retired to his cabin and, after a distressing illness, commenced his walk over the path he saw in vision—Handsome Lake had gone home to the sky-world of his fathers, and to the Creator of us all.

In 1820, after the scene was set and the American Indians prepared, the Savior and his Father appeared to Joseph Smith and ushered in the last and final dispensation of time. Shortly thereafter, the gold plates with the history of the Nephites were entrusted to his care by the Angel Moroni, the last Nephite prophet to have charge over them—"an angel from heaven, declaring glad tidings from Cumorah, for in fulfillment of the prophets, a book was to be revealed—the Book of Mormon" (see Doctrine and Covenants 128:20).

(The interesting story of Handsome Lake can be found in Arthur C. Parker's account, *The Code of Handsome Lake, the Seneca Prophet,* put together in 1913.)

—◌ 32 ◌—

The American Indian
and the Book of Mormon

Much has happened in the New World since the days of European colonization. The ancient writings of the early inhabitants of the western hemisphere are finally being deciphered, and new archaeological evidence continues to surface that paint a far different picture of the ancient people of the Americas than what was presented in the past. For instance, Frank Joseph instructs us that in July 2001, the world's leading authorities on the Maya civilization convened for a conference near Copan. Professional archaeologists and anthropologists from the United States, Mexico, El Salvador, Guatemala, Brazil, Australia, and Japan addressed an audience of 350 academic colleagues. Honduras's first Copan Congress illuminated the dark world of the Maya and revealed a people who made great cultural achievements but displayed equally great cruelty. After deciphering numerous Mayan inscriptions, modern translators have a different opinion of the Maya. Rather than a civilization of peaceful and gentle people, "their hieroglyphics paint a far different picture of incessant warfare between rival cities and the worst excesses of ritualized torture."[1]

Although Nephite and Lamanite blood may have been sprinkled among the Maya after centuries of trade, migration, and intermarriage, the root-stock of the Maya were not the Nephites. Nor were the Nahuas of Mexico, although they too were steeped in pagan philosophies, including human sacrifice. After years of researching the native races of the Americas and writing his own extensive five-volume work on the subject, Hubert Howe Bancroft concluded that the Nahuas were an idolatrous people.

He said:

> The character of the Nahuas, although the statements of the best authors are nearly unanimous concerning it, is in itself strangely contradictory. We are told that they were extremely frugal in their habits, that wealth had no attractions for them, yet we find them trafficking in the most shrewd and careful manner, delighting in splendid pageants, gorgeous dresses, and rich armor, and wasting their substance in costly feasts; they were mild with their slaves, and ferocious with their captives; they were a joyous race, fond of feasting, dancing, jesting, and innocent amusements, yet they delighted in human sacrifices and were cannibals; they possessed a well advanced civilization, yet every action of their lives was influenced by gross superstition, by a religion inconceivably dark, and bloody, and utterly without one redeeming feature; they were brave warriors, and terrible in war, yet servile and submissive to their superiors; they had a strong imagination and, in some instance, good taste, yet, they represented their gods as monsters, and their religious myths and historical legends are absurd, disgusting, and puerile.[2]

The introduction of Christianity into the region rescued the native populations from their past idolatry and prepared future generations for still further light and knowledge. Blood ties to the house of Israel, whether through Dan or those of Lehi and Mulek, and likely others, gave them an advantage, for the Savior's flock will ultimately hear his voice and follow.

Ties to Israel were more pronounced in America. Two prominent lines arrived with Lehi and Mulek, one holding the birthright in Israel and the other the scepter through Judah. It is not surprising that so many Hebrew traditions show up among the native North American tribes. So prevalent are their obvious ties to Israel that dozens of books have been written on the subject.

James Adair, who spent many years among the eastern tribes, especially the Cherokee, explains just how different they were from the pagan tribes of the world. He said:

> The ancient heathens, it is well known, worshiped a plurality of gods, gods which they formed to themselves according to their own liking, as various as the countries they inhabited, and as numerous with some as the days of the years. But these Indian Americans pay their religious devoir to . . . "the great, beneficent, supreme, holy spirit of fire," who resides (as they think) above the clouds, and on earth also with unpolluted people. He is with them the sole author of warmth, light, and of all animal and vegetable life. They do not pay the least perceivable adoration to any images, or to dead persons; neither to the celestial luminaries, nor evil spirits, nor any created being whatsoever. They are utter strangers to all the gestures practiced by the pagans in their religious rites. They kiss no idols. . . . The ceremonies of the Indians are more after the Mosaic institution, than of pagan imitation, which could not be, if the majority of the old natives were of heathen descent.[3]

Adair noted so many Hebrew traditions among the American Indians that those who read his books on the subject often accused him of being a romantic and thus not to be taken seriously. Yet he was not alone in his observations. Others came to the same conclusion, such as William W. Warren, who spent many years among the Ojibway branch of the Algonquins. Warren claims to have learned enough about their religious rites, which are kept quite secret from white men, to strengthen his belief in their analogy to the Hebrews, with their rules of life bearing a strong likeness to the Ten Commandments revealed by the Almighty to the children of Israel on Mt. Sinai.[4]

Their presence in America also ties them to the promised land referred to in the Book of Mormon. Far too many scriptures describe the greatness of the latter-day Gentile nation to have any questions about the location of the promised land any longer. The Prophet Joseph Fielding Smith tells us the Lord raised up such honorable men to assure this land remain a land of freedom. He said:

> The founders of this nation were men of humble faith. Many of them saw in vision a glorious destiny for our government, provided we would faithfully continue in the path of justice and right with contrite spirits and humble hearts, accepting the divine truths which are found in the Holy Scriptures. The appeal of these men has echoed down the passing years with prophetic warning to the succeeding generations, pleading with them to be true to all these standards which lay at the foundation of our government.
>
> This country was founded as a Christian nation, with the acceptance of Jesus Christ as the redeemer of the world. It was predicted by a prophet of old that this land would be a land of liberty and would be fortified against all other nations as long as its inhabitants would serve Jesus Christ; but would they stray from the Son of God, it would cease to be a land of liberty and his anger be kindled against them.[5]

Just as it was in days of old, living in the land of promise carries with it the responsibility to remember the Lord our God and to live righteously upon the land. This great land of liberty cannot stand without the blessings of the Almighty. But, most important, is his council to remember him, because those who forget the Lord, or set him at naught, will surely fall. The destruction of both the Nephites and Jaredites is ample evidence of his seriousness about the matter. It is no wonder such emphases is placed on reading the Book of Mormon. Within its pages we find prophetic warnings for  our day, especially in respect to defiling the promised land. From the beginning, this land was destined to rise with an influx of pilgrims from many nations under the care of founding fathers who would formulate a constitution of the people, by the people, and for the people.

Our own history books are filled with instances of success by those who had God on their side. For example, those who fought to preserve the freedom to worship Almighty God, such as the men who fought during the Revolutionary War, were spared and ultimately went on to build a nation that prospered beyond all other nations on earth. The last generations of the Nephites and Jaredites, who fought only for worldly gain, power, and possessions, lost their final battles and were consigned to the arms of Mother Earth to await a day of reconciliation. A constant study of the rise and fall of the Nephites and Jaredites can be a powerful tool in learning from the past the course we should take today. More often than not, the trials of today are simply a repeat of those of yesterday. The stories in the Book of Mormon reveal what happened to those who forgot the Lord. Only the Lamanites remained, who, regardless of their rebellious ways, were more righteous than the Nephites.

Throughout this work I have tried to identify many of

Pocahontas saving John Smith

the tribes who descended from the merged companies of Lehi and Mulek—chiefly, the Iroquois, the Cherokee and the Algonquin tribes—and how they fit into the picture during both ancient and colonial times. Many prominent American Indians have Nephite blood, something we should be aware of. The first American Indian to greet our Pilgrim Fathers on the rocky coast of Massachusetts were the Algonquins. The tribes who met William Penn were of Algonquin stock. Pocahontas was of Algonquin stock. But where are the American Indians today? Even their names are all but forgotten. William Warren wonders if someday the Lord will demand an accounting from the settlers, saying, as he did when he asked Cain "Where is Abel, thy brother?" Will he say, "Where is thy brother, and what hast thou done with him?"

In the 1845 Proclamation of the Twelve Apostles, the apostles declared that God will ultimately assemble the natives: "The remnants of Joseph in America, and make of them a great, and strong, and powerful nation. The despised and degraded son of the forest, who has wandered in dejection and sorrow, and suffered reproach, shall then drop his disguise and stand forth in manly dignity, and exclaim to the Gentiles who have envied and sold him—'I am Joseph, does my father yet live?' or in other words, I am a descendant of that Joseph who was sold into Egypt. You have hated me, and sold me and thought I was dead: but lo! I live!"

Although Lehi and Mulek's children have long since melted into the mainstream of America, the time will come when they will know who their ancient fathers were and one day will stand proudly in the shade of that Zion to come and proclaiming, "We too are Israel!"

⟶ Notes ⟶

Introduction

1. Ezra Taft Benson, *This Nation Shall Endure* (Salt Lake City: Deseret Book, 1977), 13.
2. Vincent Coon, *Choice Above All Other Lands*, 72

1—Ancient Mariners

1. Walter Beaucum, "Ancient Phoenicians in America," The Hope of Israel, http://www.uhcg.org/Lost-10-Tribes/walt3a-Phonecia.html.
2. "The Los Lunas Decalogue Stone," Los Lunas NM Decalogue Inscription, accessed Feb. 10, 2012, http://www.econ.ohio-state.edu/jhn/arch/loslunas.html.
3. Barry Fell, *America B.C.* (Muskogee: Artisan Publishers, 1989), 89–90.
4. Gene D. Matlock, *India Once Ruled the Americas!* (San Jose: Writer's Showcase), 103.

2—America's Celtic Immigrants

1. Boren and Boren, *Following the Ark of the Covenant* (Springville, UT: Bonneville Books, 2000), 37.

2. Fell, *America B.C.*, 6.
3. Ibid., 193.
4. H. H. Bancroft, *Native Races*, vol. 5, (San Francisco: A. L. Bancroft, 1883), 232.
5. Joan Elliot Price, "Ancient Sauk, Ojibway and Winnebago Cosmology: Myth, Mounds and Artifacts; A Theory of Native American Ancestral Diffusion," *Ancient American*, 22.

3—Prince Votan's Early Maya

1. L. Taylor Hansen, *The Ancient Atlantic* (Amherst: Palmer Publications, 1969), 365.
2. Josiah Priest, *American Antiquities* (Albany: Hoffman & White, 1838), 326.
3. Fell, *America B.C.*, 311.
4. Frank Joseph, *Survivors of Atlantis* (Rochester: Bear & Company, 2004), 190.
5. William F. McNeil, *Visitors to Ancient America* (Jefferson: McFarland, 2005), 94.
6. Robert B. Stacy Judd, *Atlantis, Mother of Empire*, (Kempton: Adventures Unlimited Press), 28.
7. Andrew Collins, "Is Cuba the Lost Island of Atlantis," *Ancient American,* no. 38, 11–12.
8. Hansen, *The Ancient Atlantic*, 134.
9. Ibid., 366.
10. Ibid., 48.

5—Lehi's Land of Promise

1. Joseph Smith Jr., *The Personal Writings of Joseph Smith*, 344–46.
2. Bruce R. McConkie, *Mormon Doctrine* (Salt Lake City: Bookcraft, 1966), 306.
3. Ezra Taft Benson, *The Teachings of Ezra Taft Benson* (Salt Lake City: Bookcraft, 1988), 578.
4. Ezra Taft Benson, "Our Divine Constitution," *Ensign*, Nov. 1987.

7—Defining Book of Mormon Territory

1. H. L. Fairchild, *Geologic Story of the Genesee Valley and Western New York* (Rochester: published by author, 1928), 140.
2. Ibid., 141.

3. W. A. Richie, *Indian History of New York State, Part 3—The Algonkian Tribe* (Albany: New York State Museum and Science Service), 5.

8—Zarahemla

1. Hugh Nibley, *An Approach to the Book of Mormon: A Course of Study for the Melchizedek Priesthood Quorums of The Church of Jesus Christ of Latter-day Saints* (first edition, 1957), 431.
2. E. G. Squire, *Aboriginal Monuments of the State of New York* (published in the *Smithsonian Contributions to Knowledge,* vol. II) Oct. 20, 1848, 73.
3. Ibid., 71.

9—Bountiful

1. Squire, *Aboriginal Monuments of the State of New York*,66.
2. Ibid., 79.

10—The Land Northward

1. Parker E. Calkin and Carlton E. Brett, "Ancestral Niagara River Drainage: Stratigraphic and Paleontological Setting," GSA Bulletin 89, no. 8 (Aug. 1978), 1140–54.
2. Squire, *Aboriginal Monuments of the State of New York*, 66.

11–Desolation

1. Fairchild, *Geologic Story of the Genesee Valley and Western New York*, 200.
2. Richie, *Indian History of New York State*, 5.
3. Arad Thomas, "The Holland Purchase," *The Pioneer History of Orleans County, NY*, online edition by Holice & Deb.
4. Ibid.

12—The Jaredites as Metallurgists

1. Roger Jewell, *Ancient Mines of Kitchi Gummi* (Fairfield: Jewell Histories, 2004), 6.
2. Bradford B. Van Diver, *Roadside Geology* (Missoula: Mountain Press Publishing, 1994), 282.
3. Josiah Priest, *American Antiquities* (Albany: Hoffman & White, 1838), 265.

4. Ibid., 261.

5. W. A. Ritchie, *The Archaeology of New York State,* revised edition (Garden City: American Museum of Natural History, 1965), 183.

6. Richie, *Indian History of New York State,* Educational Leaflet No. 6, 23.

7. Wilbur M. Cunningham, *A Study of the Glacial Kame Culture in Michigan, Ohio, and Indiana* (Ann Arbor: Museum of Anthropology, University of Michigan, 1978), 15.

8. Benoit Crevier, "Niagara's Ancient Cemetery of Giants" (Toronto: *Daily Telegraph,* 1871), 1; republished in *Ancient American,* issue 41, 9.

9. Ibid.

13—The Merged Nephite and Mulekite Populations

1. Davidly Yair, *Lost Israelite Identity,* 161.

2. Ritchie, *The Archaeology of New York State,* 208.

14—The Iroquois/Algonquin Connection

1. Ritchie, *The Archaeology of New York State,* 241.

2. William Warren, *History of the Ojibway People* (St. Paul: published in 1885 by the Minnesota Historical Society as vol. 5 of the *Collections of the Minnesota Historical Society,* reprinted in 1984), 63.

3. "Proto-Algonquin Language," Wikipedia, http://en.wikipedia.org/wiki/Proto-Algonquian_language.

4. Cyclone Covey, "Are Today's Cherokee Descendants of America's First Civilizers?" *Ancient American* 56, 22.

5. Don Dragoo, in Joseph R. Caldwell and Robert L. Hall, eds, *Hopewellian Studies* (Springfield, IL: Illinois State Museum, 1964), 16.

6. "Haplogroup X (mtDNA)," Wikipedia, http://en.wikipedia.org/wiki/Haplogroup_X_%28mtDNA%29.

7. Ritchie, *The Archaeology of New York State,* 300.

15—Nephite-Type Writing

1. Fell, *America B.C.,* 254–64.

16—The Mound Builders

1. Dragoo, in *Hopewellian Studies,* 9.

2. "Mitochondrial DNA Analysis of the Ohio Hopewell of the Hopewell Mound Group," PhD dissertation by Lisa A. Mills, Dept. of Anthropology, Ohio State University, 2003.
3. Ibid.
4. Dragoo, in *Hopewellian Studies*, 17.
5. Ritchie, *The Archaeology of New York State,* 202.
6. Ibid., 201.
7. James Griffin, in *Hopewellian Studies*, 15.
8. Stuart Struever, "The Hopewell Interaction Sphere Riverine-Western Great Lakes Culture history," *Hopewellian Studies*, 88.
9. Edward McMichael, in *Hopewellian Studies,* 132.
10. Stephen D. Peet, *The Mound Builders* (Chicago: Office of the American Antiquarian, 1892), 263.
11. Dragoo, in *Hopewellian Studies,* 25.

17—Treasures Beneath the Mounds

1. H. C. Shetrone, *The Mound Builders* (New York: D. Appleton and Co., 1930), 43.
2. Ibid., 218.
3. Stephen D. Peet, in *The Mound Builders* (Chicago: Office of the American Antiquarian, 1892), 221.
4. Silverberg, *The Mound Builders* (Athens: Ohio University Press, 1970), 202–203.
5. Peet, *The Mound Builder*, 52.
6. Ibid., 248–49.

18—The Cherokee and Sioux Connection

1. Josiah Priest, *American Antiquities* (Albany: Hoffman & White, 1838), 220.
2. Price, "Ancient Sauk, Ojibway and Winnebago Cosmology," 42.
3. Kenneth W. Godfrey, "The Zelph Story," BYU Studies (Spring 1989): 5.
4. Price, "Ancient Sauk, Ojibway and Winnebago Cosmology," 10.
5. J. W. Powell, "Mounds of the Kanawha Valley, W. V.," in *Ancient American 79*, 24–28.

21–The Time of Christ

1. John Matthew Thekkel, MA, PhD, "A Brief History of India," www .thekkel.com/indiahh.html

22—The Post Christian Era & Decline

1. Roger Kennedy, *Hidden Cities* (New York: The Free Press, 1994), 16
2. Ibid., 67.
3. Isabel Hill Elder, *Celt, Druid and Culdee* (Muskogee: Hoffman Printing, 1990), 59.
4. Ibid., 94.
5. Ibid., 96.
6. Ritchie, *The Archaeology of New York State*, 216.
7. Kennedy, *Hidden Cities* (New York: The Free Press, 1994), 267.
8. Olaf H. Pruffer, in *Hopewellian Studies*, 54.
9. Stuart Struever, in *Hopewellian Studies*, 88.

23—The Fall of the Ohio Hopewell

1. John D. Baldwin, *Ancient America in Notes on American Archaeology* (Montana: Kessinger Publishing, 1872), 201.
2. Hubert Howe Bancroft, *The Native Races,* vol. 5 (San Francisco: A. L. Bancroft & Company, 1883), 210–11.
3. J. W. Foster, *Prehistoric Races* (Chicago: S. C. Griggs & Company, 1873), 341–42.
4. Baldwin, *Ancient America,* 202.

25—Footprints of a Vanished Race

1. E. Cecil McGavin and Willard Bean, *The Geography of the Book of Mormon* (Salt Lake City: Bookcraft, 1949), 63.
2. Ibid., 87.
3. Ibid., 84–85.
4. B. H. Roberts, *New Witness for God,* vol. 3 (Salt Lake City: Deseret News, 1951), 73.
5. Brigham Young Jr., *The Millennial Star,* Aug. 19, 1873, (33): 513-16), in John Heinerman, *Hidden Treasures of Ancient American Cultures* (Springville: CFI, 2001), 46.
6. Brigham Young, *Journal of Discourses,* vol. 19 (Islington, William Budge, 1878), 38.
7. Joseph Fielding Smith, *Doctrines of Salvation,* vol. 3 (Salt Lake City: Bookcraft, 1956), 240–41.
8. Ibid., 233, 234.
9. Joseph Smith, the Wentworth Letter, *History of the Church,* vol. 4 (Salt Lake: Deseret Book, 1949), 537.

10. Fell, *America B.C.,* 107.

26–Further Cleansing

1. Hubert Howe Bancroft, *The Native Races*, vol. 5 (San Francisco: A. L. Bancroft & Company, 1883), 245.
2. Ibid., 248.
3. Ibid., 285.
4. Ibid.
5. Ibid., 292.
6. Ibid., 285.

27—The Mississippi Culture

1. John McIntosh, *The Origins of the North American Indians* (Pearl St. Safis & Cornish, 1843), 205.
2. Conant, *Footprints of Vanished Races* (St. Lewis: Chancy R. Barns, 1879), 59–60.
3. *Journal of Discourses*, vol. 8, 344.

28—Lamanite Migrations

1. Heckewelder, *History Manners, and Customs of the Indian Nations*, 74. Repeated in David McCutchen, *The Red Record* (Garden Park: Avery Publishing Group, 1989), 42–43.

31—The Iroquois Prophet, Handsome Lake

1. Morgan, 234; Arthur C. Parker, "Code of Handsome Lake, the Seneca Prophet," http://www.sacred-texts.com/nam/iro/parkercho 1002.htm.

32—The American Indians and the Book of Mormon

1. Frank Joseph, "Latest Discoveries Show the Maya in a New Light," *Ancient American* 41, 37–39.
2. H. H. Bancroft, *Native Races*, vol. 2 (San Francisco: A.L. Bancroft & Company, 1883), 626.
3. James Adair, *The History of the American Indians*, 20–21.
4. Ibid., 67.
5. Joseph Fielding Smith, *Doctrines of Salvation*, vol. III, 325.

⸺ Partial Bibilography ⸻

Baldwin, John D. *Ancient America*. New York: Harper and Brothers, 1872.

Cunningham, Wilbur M. *A Study of the Glacial Kame Culture in Michigan, Ohio, and Indiana*. Ann Arbor: University of Michigan Press, 1948.

Caldwell, Joseph R. & Hall, Robert L. Editors. *Hopewellian Studies*. State of Illinois: Illinois State Museum, 1964.

Dragoo, Don. *Mounds for the Dead: An Analysis of the Adena Culture*, vol. 37. Pittsburgh, PA: Annals of Carnegie Museum, 1964, 1971.

Fairchild, Herman LeRoy. *Geologic Story of the Genesee Valley and Western New York*. New York: Scrantoms, 1928.

Fell, Barry. *America B. C.*, Artisan Publishers, 1989.

Gordon, Cyrus, H. *Before Columbus*. New York: Crown Publishers, 1971.

Hansen, L. Taylor. *He Walked the Americas*. Amherst, Wisconsin: Legend Press, 1953.

Hansen, Vaughn E. *Whence Came They*. Springville, UT: CFI, 1993.

Hunter, Milton R. *Archaeology and the Book of Mormon*. Salt Lake City: Deseret Book, 1956.

Kennedy, Roger G. *Hidden Cities*. New York: Macmillan, 1994.

McGavin, E. C. & Bean, W. *The Geography of the Book of Mormon*, Salt Lake City: Bookcraft, 1949.

McIntosh, John. *The Origins of the North American Indians*. New York: Nafis & Cornish, 1843.

McNeil, William F. *Visitors to Ancient America*. McFarland & Co., 2005.

Peet, Stephen D. *The Mound Builders*, Office of the American Antiquarian, 1892.

Priest, Josiah. *American Antiquities and Discoveries in the West*. Hoffman & White, 1838.

Ritchie, William A. *The Archaeology of New York State*. Garden City, NY: The Natural History Press, Garden City, 1965.

Silverberg, Robert. *The Mound Builders*. Athens, Ohio: Ohio University Press, 1970.

Smith, Joseph Fielding. *Doctrines of Salvation*, vols. I, II, III, Salt Lake City: Bookcraft, 1955.

Stephens, John L. esq. *Incidents of Travel in Central America, Chiapas and Yucatan*, vol. 1 & 11, New York: Harper & Brothers, 1850.

Squire, E. G. *Antiquities of the State of New York.* Buffalo, New York: Geo. H. Derby & Co., 1851.

Squire & Davies. *Ancient Monuments of the Mississippi Valley,* New York: Bartlett & Welford.

‑ Index ‑

—ᴄ ABOUT THE AUTHOR ᴄ—

Phyllis C. Olive lives in Las Vegas, Nevada, with her husband and best friend, Ron Olive. They have a combined family of seven children, seventeen grandchildren, and ten great-grand-children. Her various talents include art (her paintings hang in many homes), music, and history. Being confined to her home by a long, lingering illness, Phyllis has had ample time to study the scriptures and the history of nations in hopes of gaining a little better understanding of just what caused their rise to power and their ultimately fall from grace, especially those affiliated with the Book of Mormon, which she loves. It appears the Nephites were not alone in the land. Thus, her research took her into many lands as she followed various people from their places of origin into the world of the Book of Mormon. It has been a difficult journey for her. Pain and debilitating fatigue was her constant companion as she gained each new piece of information and slowly wove together a tapestry of history that adds new color and insights into the world of both the Nephites and Jaredites. Now that it is done, will she stop? No, new and exciting ideas are still dancing around in her head.